Better Homes and Gardens®

Crockery Cooker
Cook Book

© 1976 by Meredith Corporation, Des Moines, Iowa.
All Rights Reserved. Printed in the United States of America.
First Edition. Sixth Printing, 1978.
Library of Congress Catalog Card Number: 75-40624
ISBN: 0-696-00860-2

On the cover: Long, slow simmering in a crockery cooker is a great convenience idea, especially for those who are away from home all day. Accompany *Vegetable-Topped Rump Roast* with hot bread and beverage for a tasty meal (see recipe, page 11).

Above: Keep your cooker handy where you can use it often. Don't limit it to basic cooking jobs. Try these exciting recipes—*Holiday Carrot Pudding* (see recipe, page 77), *Fruit Compote Supreme* (see recipe, page 49), or *Flaming Punch* (see recipe, page 90).

Contents

BETTER HOMES AND GARDENS BOOKS
Editorial Director: Don Dooley
Managing Editor: Malcolm E. Robinson   Art Director: John Berg
Asst. Managing Editor: Lawrence D. Clayton   Asst. Art Director: Randall Yontz
Food Editor: Nancy Morton
Senior Food Editor: Joyce Trollope
Associate Editors: Sandra Granseth, Sharyl Heiken, Rosemary C. Hutchinson, Elizabeth Strait
Assistant Editors: Flora Elliott, Diane Nelson
Designers: Harijs Priekulis, Faith Berven, Candy Carleton
Technical Consultant: Agnes Frances Carlin, Ph.D., Iowa State University

Our seal assures you that every recipe in *Crockery Cooker Cook Book* is endorsed by the Better Homes and Gardens Test Kitchen. Each recipe is tested for family appeal, practicality, and deliciousness.

Crockery Cookery Know-How

Dinner that cooks by itself is a dream come true to the user of electric slow-crockery cookers. The go-off-and-leave-it feature alone is responsible for much of the appliance's popularity. The big question is, "go off and leave it—for how long?" The answer depends both on the type of cooker and on the food.

Meet the Crockery Cookers: Although individual models have different features, slow cookers come in three basic types. Cookers with heating wires wrapped entirely around the sides of the cooker, those with heating elements in the bottom, and those with a separate heating unit like a small hot plate.

We tested the recipes for this book **only** in those cookers with heating elements wrapped around the sides (*illustration* **1**).* These pots have very low wattage and the element is on continuously. Foods in liquid can be left unattended 8 or more hours without boiling dry or sticking. This group of pots can be identified by the heat control with one or two fixed settings, a Low and High.

The second group, with heating elements in the bottom, usually have thermostatic controls with a wide range of temperatures (*illustration* **2**). The heating unit goes on and off as the thermostat calls for heat. In some models the settings on the dial range from very low to high enough for deep fat frying. Slow cooking in crockery cookers heated from the bottom is most successful when the user can check the food during cooking to be sure it is hot enough or not boiling too hard. An occasional stir also prevents food from sticking to the bottom or sides of the cooker. If you have one of these models, you should not use the recipes in the All-Day Cooking chapter unless you plan to be at home during the cooking time. We did not test recipes either in the second group of cookers or in those with a separate heating unit which operates much like a hot plate (*illustration* **3**). In addition to the example shown, some models are shallow like a skillet. The change in shape also affects the heating pattern of the appliance.

Check Your Cooker: Just as the design of the slow cooker varies so does its heating capacity. To check the cooking temperature of your particular cooker, fill it half full of cold tap water. Cover and set cooker on high-heat setting for 2½ hours. If the water is boiling before 2½ hours, reduce the total cooking time for recipes in this book. If the cooker takes longer than 3 hours to come to boiling, add to the cooking time.

Food Safety First: Slow cookers are designed for long cooking periods. Thus, the food heats very slowly particularly on the lowest setting. It follows that Low should not be used for meat or egg mixtures

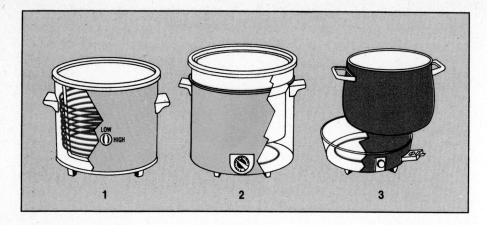

1   2   3

that cook less than 6 hours. The food won't get hot enough in that amount of time to be sure of destroying bacteria.

Proper handling of foods before and after cooking is another important aspect of crockery cooking. Don't use the cooker to store food at room temperature either before or after cooking. While you'll want to do some advance preparation the night before, you must store the ingredients in the refrigerator and transfer them to the cooker in the morning. Likewise, as soon as the meal is served, remove the food from the cooker. Refrigerate the food while still warm, or cool it over a bowl of ice water and freeze or store in the refrigerator.

Useful Tips: Before using the crockery cooker for the first time, read the instruction booklet so you can learn about specific features. As you use the cooker you may find it becomes hot to the touch during the long cooking time. Use heavy potholders to move the cooker and place the cord so it will not hang over the counter where it can be touched or tangled accidentally.

Sudden temperature changes will damage the ceramic liner of the cooker. Thus, never put cold food or water in a hot cooker. Turn on the cooker only after foods are in the pot. Also, never place the cooker in the refrigerator because condensation on the electrical parts may interfere with the proper performance.

Unless the instruction book says the pot is immersible, do not plunge the cooker in water. Avoid abrasive cleaners and cleaning pads. Scratches in the liner can trap food particles that never completely come out. For easiest clean up, add warm water to the cooker just after removing the food.

From the beginning of the book to the end, you will discover exciting crockery cooking recipes for any occasion.

Rival Crock Pot, Hamilton Beach Crock Watcher, Sears Crockery Cooker, Penneys Slow Crockery Cooker, Lady Vanity Potpourri Crock, and Grandinetti Crockery Cook Pot.

All-Day Cooking

(More Than 8 Hours)

Low heat is the answer to cooking delicious *Savory Beef-Vegetable Soup* (see recipe, page 36). Generously ladle the soup into bowls for a hearty supper. Crusty bread with melted cheese complements the soup.

Plug in a crockery cooker and start enjoying meals cooked the easy way. Once the food goes into the pot, the food cooks many hours, sometimes for 12 hours, depending on the recipe. You can even leave the crockery cooker operating while you are away from home all day. On the following pages you'll find a wide collection of taste-tempting main dishes, soups, and stews to please the heartiest of appetites. There are also recipes in this section for steaming hot vegetables and delicious fruit desserts to fix in the morning to serve for the evening meal.

Slow Cooking Main Dishes

MARINATED FLANK FILLETS

1 1-pound beef flank steak
1 cup sliced onion
¾ cup apple cider
½ teaspoon coarsely ground
    pepper

8 slices bacon
    Cooking oil
1 9-ounce package frozen
    artichoke hearts
    Herbed Hollandaise Sauce

Pound meat with meat mallet to even thickness. Cut lengthwise into six 1-inch strips. Cut *two* of the strips in half. In bowl combine onion, cider, and pepper. Add meat; stir to coat. Cover; refrigerate overnight. Turn meat twice.

Drain meat; reserve marinade. Sprinkle strips with salt. Roll *1½* strips jelly-roll fashion, starting with short sides; repeat. Tie or skewer securely. Place meat in crockery cooker; add marinade. Cover; cook on low-heat setting for 10 hours. Remove meat; discard marinade. Remove string or skewers. In skillet cook bacon just till done, but not crisp.

Wrap *two* slices around each meat roll; secure with picks. Place on broiler pan; brush tops lightly with oil. Broil meat 3 inches from heat for 2½ to 3 minutes.

Cook artichoke hearts following package directions; drain. Serve with meat. Spoon Herbed Hollandaise Sauce atop each roll; pass remaining. Serves 4.

Herbed Hollandaise Sauce: Prepare 1 envelope hollandaise sauce mix according to package directions *except* use 1¼ cups milk. Stir in 2 tablespoons chopped green onion with tops; ½ teaspoon dried tarragon, crushed; and ¼ teaspoon dried chervil, crushed. Makes about 1⅓ cups.

SAUCY STEAK ROLLS

Trim fat from one 1½-pound beef round steak, cut ¼ inch thick. Pound meat very thin; cut into 8 equal rectangular pieces. Sprinkle with salt and pepper. Combine ¼ cup finely chopped onion; 2 tablespoons snipped parsley; and ½ teaspoon dried basil, crushed. Divide between meat pieces. Roll jelly-roll fashion, starting with short sides; tuck edges in around stuffing. Tie or skewer

securely. Coat with 2 tablespoons all-purpose flour. In skillet brown in 2 tablespoons hot cooking oil; drain. Place in crockery cooker. Combine one 10¾-ounce can condensed cream of mushroom soup, ¼ cup catsup, and 1 teaspoon Worcestershire sauce; pour over meat. Cover; cook on low-heat setting for 8 to 10 hours. Remove cord or skewers. Pass sauce. Serves 6 to 8.

Ten-hour cooking makes entertaining easy, especially if you're gone all day. When you return, remove *Marinated Flank Fillets* from the crockery cooker, wrap with bacon and slip under the oven broiler.

HERBED ROUND STEAK

A little advance preparation makes this dinner ready to eat when the cook comes home—

1 2-pound beef round steak,
  cut ¾ inch thick
¼ cup all-purpose flour
½ teaspoon salt
⅛ teaspoon pepper
2 tablespoons cooking oil
1 medium onion, sliced

1 10¾-ounce can condensed cream
  of celery soup
½ teaspoon dried oregano,
  crushed
¼ teaspoon dried thyme, crushed
⅓ cup cold water
3 tablespoons all-purpose flour

Trim fat from steak. Cut meat into 6 equal pieces. Coat meat pieces in ¼ cup flour; pound both sides with meat mallet. Sprinkle with salt and pepper. In skillet brown steaks on both sides in hot oil; drain, reserving 1 tablespoon drippings. Place meat in crockery cooker. Cook onion in reserved drippings; stir in soup, oregano, and thyme. Spoon mixture over steaks. Cover; cook on low-heat setting for 8 to 10 hours. Measure 1½ cups cooking liquid into saucepan. Blend ⅓ cup cold water slowly into 3 tablespoons flour; stir into liquid. Cook and stir till thickened and bubbly. Season to taste. Serves 6.

MEXICAN FLANK STEAK

2 1-pound beef flank steaks
⅛ teaspoon garlic salt
1 15-ounce can tamales in sauce
1 teaspoon instant beef
  bouillon granules

1 8-ounce can tomato sauce
  Dash bottled hot pepper sauce
2 tablespoons cold water
4 teaspoons cornstarch
  Shredded Monterey Jack cheese

Pound meat on both sides with meat mallet; sprinkle with garlic salt, ½ teaspoon salt, and ⅛ teaspoon pepper. Unwrap tamales; place tamales and sauce in bowl. Break up tamales slightly with fork; spread over steaks. Roll up each steak jelly-roll fashion, starting with short side; tie or skewer securely. Place in crockery cooker. Dissolve bouillon in ¼ cup hot water; combine with tomato sauce and hot pepper sauce. Pour over meat. Cover; cook on low-heat setting for 8 to 10 hours. Lift out meat rolls; remove strings or skewers. Pour cooking liquid into saucepan; skim off excess fat. Blend 2 tablespoons cold water into cornstarch; stir into liquid. Cook and stir till thickened and bubbly. Spoon over meat; sprinkle cheese atop each roll. Serves 6.

TEST KITCHEN TIP—ALL COOKERS ARE NOT ALIKE

Remember, these recipes were tested only in the 3½- to 4-quart crockery cookers that have the heating element wrapped around a crockery liner. If you have a different type of cooker, you may need to adjust the timing of recipes and to stir the food occasionally. See pages 4 and 5 for more information.

MARINATED POT ROAST DINNER

1 3-pound beef chuck pot roast
1½ cups tomato juice
¼ cup wine vinegar
1 clove garlic, minced
2 teaspoons Worcestershire
    sauce
1½ teaspoons salt
1 teaspoon sugar

½ teaspoon dried basil, crushed
½ teaspoon dried thyme, crushed
¼ teaspoon pepper
6 small onions, halved
1 cup chopped carrot
½ cup cold water
¼ cup all-purpose flour

Advance Preparation: Trim excess fat from roast. If necessary, cut roast in halves or thirds to fit in crockery cooker. Place meat in plastic bag; set in deep bowl. Stir together tomato juice, wine vinegar, minced garlic, Worcestershire sauce, salt, sugar, basil, thyme, and pepper. Pour marinade over meat; close bag. Marinate overnight in refrigerator, turning twice.

Before serving: In crockery cooker place onions and carrot. Place roast atop vegetables; add marinade. Cover and cook on low-heat setting for 8 to 10 hours. Remove roast and vegetables. Skim off excess fat from cooking liquid. Measure 2 cups cooking liquid; pour into saucepan. Return meat and vegetables to cooker; cover to keep warm. Blend ½ cup cold water slowly into ¼ cup flour; stir into cooking liquid. Cook and stir till mixture is thickened and bubbly. Place meat on a warm serving platter; top with vegetables. Pour some of the gravy over; pass the remaining gravy. Makes 6 servings.

VEGETABLE-TOPPED RUMP ROAST

Dinner is easy with this favorite meat-vegetable combination (shown on the cover)—

2 tablespoons all-purpose flour
½ teaspoon salt
¼ teaspoon paprika
    Dash pepper
1 2-pound boneless beef rump
    roast, rolled and tied
2 tablespoons cooking oil
12 small potatoes, peeled
6 medium carrots, diced

2 medium onions, sliced (1 cup)
½ green pepper, cut in pieces
1 10½-ounce can vegetable
    beef soup
¼ cup water
1 bay leaf
⅓ cup cold water (optional)
3 tablespoons all-purpose flour
    (optional)

Combine the 2 tablespoons flour, salt, paprika, and pepper; coat roast with mixture. In heavy skillet brown roast on all sides in hot oil. In crockery cooker place the potatoes, carrots, onions, and green pepper. Place roast atop vegetables. Combine soup, ¼ cup water, and bay leaf; pour over roast. Cover and cook on low-heat setting for 10 to 12 hours. To serve, discard the bay leaf and remove strings from meat. Arrange the meat and vegetables on serving platter. Spoon some of the soup mixture atop. If thicker gravy is desired, in saucepan blend ⅓ cup cold water slowly into 3 tablespoons flour; stir in soup mixture. Cook and stir till thickened and bubbly. Makes 6 servings.

SAUERBRATEN

In a large bowl combine 1½ cups Burgundy; 1½ cups red wine vinegar; 2 medium onions, sliced; ½ lemon, sliced; 12 whole cloves; 6 bay leaves; 6 whole peppercorns; 1 tablespoon sugar; 1 tablespoon salt; and ¼ teaspoon ground ginger. Add one 3- to 4-pound beef rump roast; turn to coat. Cover; refrigerate about 36 hours. Turn meat at least twice daily. Remove meat; wipe dry.

Strain and reserve marinade. In skillet brown meat on all sides in 2 tablespoons hot shortening; drain. Place in crockery cooker; add marinade. Cover; cook on low-heat setting for 8 to 10 hours. Remove meat. Measure 1¼ cups cooking liquid into saucepan. Add ¾ cup water and ⅔ cup broken gingersnaps. Cook and stir till sauce is thickened. Serve with roast. Serves 8 to 10.

SOUR-CREAMED POT ROAST

2 slices bacon
1 3-pound beef chuck roast
¾ cup chopped onion
1 teaspoon salt
1 bay leaf
¼ teaspoon ground cumin

⅛ teaspoon pepper
½ cup dairy sour cream
3 tablespoons all-purpose flour
2 tablespoons snipped parsley
½ teaspoon Kitchen Bouquet
Hot cooked noodles

In skillet cook bacon till crisp; drain, reserving drippings. Crumble bacon; wrap and refrigerate. Trim fat from roast; cut in half to fit into crockery cooker. In skillet brown meat in bacon drippings; drain. Place in cooker. Stir together onion, salt, bay leaf, cumin, pepper, and ¼ cup water; pour over meat. Cover; cook on low-heat setting for 8 to 10 hours. Remove roast; discard bay leaf. Skim fat from liquid; pour liquid into saucepan. Return roast to cooker; cover. Blend sour cream and flour; stir into hot liquid. Cook and stir till thickened; do not boil. Stir in parsley and Kitchen Bouquet. Season to taste. Serve meat garnished with bacon. Serve gravy over noodles. Serves 6.

CARROT-PINEAPPLE ROAST DINNER

In crockery cooker place 1 cup thinly sliced carrots. Trim excess fat from one 3-pound beef chuck pot roast; cut in half and fit into cooker atop carrots. Sprinkle with salt and pepper. Combine one 8¼-ounce can crushed pineapple, undrained; 2 tablespoons brown sugar, 2 tablespoons soy sauce; 1 clove garlic, minced; and ½ teaspoon dried basil, crushed. Spoon over roast. Cover; cook on low-heat setting for 8 to 10 hours. Remove roast. Drain carrots and pineapple; reserve cooking liquid. Return meat, carrots, and pineapple to cooker; cover to keep warm. Skim fat from reserved liquid. Add water to make 1¾ cups; pour into saucepan. Blend ¼ cup cold water slowly into 2 tablespoons all-purpose flour; stir into reserved liquid. Cook and stir till thickened. Place meat on serving platter; top with carrots and pineapple. Pour some of gravy over meat and hot cooked noodles; pass remaining. Makes 6 servings.

CRANBERRY POT ROAST

Trim the excess fat from one 3- to 3½-pound beef chuck pot roast; cut in half to fit into crockery cooker. In skillet brown meat in 2 tablespoons hot cooking oil; drain. Stir together one 16-ounce can whole cranberry sauce, 2 tablespoons water, 1½ teaspoons salt, and ⅛ teaspoon pepper; pour into cooker. Place meat on rack in cooker above cranberries. Cover meat loosely with foil. Cover and cook on low-heat setting for 8 to 10 hours. Remove meat. Measure 2 cups cooking liquid; pour into saucepan. Return meat to cooker; cover. Blend 2 tablespoons cold water slowly into 2 tablespoons cornstarch; stir into cooking liquid. Cook and stir till thickened and bubbly. Place meat on serving platter. Serve sauce over hot mashed potatoes. Serves 6 to 8.

ORIENTAL SWEET-SOUR POT ROAST

1 3- to 3½-pound beef chuck
   pot roast
2 tablespoons cooking oil
1 16-ounce can bean sprouts,
   rinsed and drained
1 5-ounce can water chestnuts,
   drained and thinly sliced
1 medium green pepper, cut
   in 1-inch squares
⅓ cup apricot jam
¼ cup vinegar

1 tablespoon soy sauce
1 clove garlic, minced
1 teaspoon salt
½ teaspoon ground ginger
⅛ teaspoon pepper
     ● ● ●
1 11-ounce can mandarin orange
   sections
3 tablespoons cornstarch
   Hot cooked rice

Trim excess fat from roast; cut in half to fit into crockery cooker. In skillet brown meat in hot oil; drain. Place meat in cooker; add bean sprouts, water chestnuts, and green pepper. Stir together jam, vinegar, soy, garlic, salt, ginger, and pepper. Pour over meat and vegetables. Cover; cook on low-heat setting for 8 to 10 hours. Remove meat and vegetables. Skim fat from cooking liquid. Measure 2 cups liquid; reserve. Return meat and vegetables to cooker; cover to keep warm. Drain oranges, reserving ¼ cup of the syrup. In a saucepan blend reserved syrup slowly into cornstarch; stir in reserved cooking liquid. Cook and stir till thickened and bubbly. Stir in orange sections; heat through. Season to taste. Place meat and vegetables on platter. Spoon some sauce over; pass remaining. Serve with rice. Serves 8.

TEST KITCHEN TIP—STORING COOKED FOOD

Never store leftover cooked food at room temperature in a crockery cooker. After the meal, remove any remaining food from the cooker immediately. Refrigerate food while still warm or chill over a bowl of ice water. Do not place crockery cooker in the refrigerator or use it to reheat cold food.

HOME-STYLE POT ROAST

1 medium turnip, chopped
   (½ cup)
1 medium onion, chopped
   (½ cup)
¼ cup chopped carrot
¼ cup chopped celery
1 clove garlic, minced
1 3-pound beef chuck pot
   roast

2 tablespoons cooking oil
1 teaspoon salt
¼ teaspoon pepper
½ cup red wine *or* water

. . .

2 tablespoons snipped parsley
⅓ cup cold water
3 tablespoons all-purpose flour

In a crockery cooker place the chopped turnip, onion, carrot, celery, and garlic. Trim excess fat from roast; cut in half to fit in cooker. In skillet brown the roast on all sides in hot oil; drain. Place meat atop vegetables. Sprinkle roast with salt and pepper; pour the wine or water over roast. Cover and cook on low-heat setting for 8 to 10 hours. Remove roast to a warm serving platter. Strain the vege- tables; reserve 2 cups cooking liquid, adding water if necessary. Spoon the vegetables atop roast; sprinkle with parsley. Cover meat to keep warm while preparing gravy. Skim excess fat from reserved cooking liquid; pour into sauce-pan. Blend the ⅓ cup cold water slowly into flour; stir into cooking liquid. Cook and stir till thickened and bubbly. Serve with roast and vegetables. Serves 6 to 8.

Home-Style Pot Roast is a natural choice for all-day cooking. The meat and vegetables simmer together, each enhancing the flavor of the other and leaving only one container to be washed.

STEAK WITH VEGETABLE GRAVY

¾ cup finely chopped carrot
¾ cup finely chopped onion
½ cup finely chopped celery
¼ cup finely chopped green
    pepper

1 2-pound beef round steak,
    cut ¾ inch thick
½ cup catsup
1 tablespoon vinegar
2 tablespoons all-purpose flour

In crockery cooker place carrot, onion, celery, and green pepper. Trim excess fat from meat; cut into 6 equal pieces. Place meat atop vegetables. Sprinkle with salt and pepper. Combine catsup, vinegar, and ⅓ cup water; pour over meat. Cover and cook on low-heat setting for 8 to 10 hours. Remove meat.

Skim excess fat from cooking liquid; pour mixture into saucepan. Return meat to cooker. Blend ½ cup cold water slowly into flour. Stir into vegetable mixture. Cook and stir till thickened and bubbly. Place meat on platter. Spoon some gravy over; pass remaining gravy. Serves 6 to 8.

PIZZA SWISS STEAK

Trim excess fat from one 2-pound beef round steak, cut 1 inch thick. Cut into 6 equal pieces. Stir together 2 tablespoons all-purpose flour, 2 teaspoons salt, and ¼ teaspoon pepper. Coat meat with flour mixture. Pound steak to ½-inch thickness using meat mallet. In skillet brown meat in 2 tablespoons hot cooking oil; drain off fat. Place 1 medium onion, thinly sliced and separated into rings in crockery cooker. Place meat atop. Stir together one 8-ounce can tomato sauce, one 8-ounce can pizza sauce, ½ cup water, ½ teaspoon sugar, and ½ teaspoon dried oregano, crushed; pour over meat. Cover; cook on low-heat setting for 8 to 10 hours. Serve over hot cooked spaghetti. Serves 6.

DEVILED STEAK CUBES

1 1½-pound beef round steak,
    cut ¾ inch thick
2 tablespoons cooking oil
½ cup tomato sauce
½ cup chopped onion
    (1 medium)
2 tablespoons vinegar
1 tablespoon prepared mustard

2 teaspoons prepared
    horseradish
1 clove garlic, minced
¾ teaspoon salt
¼ teaspoon pepper
⅔ cup cold water
⅓ cup all-purpose flour
    Hot cooked noodles

Trim excess fat from meat; cut meat into cubes. In skillet brown meat on all sides in hot oil; drain. Transfer meat to crockery cooker. Stir in tomato sauce, onion, vinegar, mustard, horseradish, garlic, salt, pepper, and 1 cup water.

Cover; cook on low-heat setting for 8 to 10 hours. Turn to high-heat setting. Blend cold water slowly into flour; stir into meat mixture. Cook till thickened; stir occasionally. Serve over noodles. Makes 6 servings.

STUFFED FLANK STEAK

¼ cup chopped celery
¼ cup chopped onion
2 tablespoons butter *or*
    margarine
⅓ cup water

1 cup corn bread stuffing mix
1 1-pound beef flank steak
2 tablespoons cooking oil
1 10¾-ounce can golden
    mushroom soup

In saucepan cook celery and onion in butter till tender but not brown. Add water; bring to boiling. Stir in stuffing mix; remove from heat. Score steak on one side, making diamond-shaped cuts. Spread stuffing over unscored side of meat. Roll up jelly-roll fashion, starting with short side; tie or skewer securely. In skillet brown steak roll on all sides in hot oil; drain. Transfer to crockery cooker; season with salt and pepper. Spoon soup over meat. Cover and cook on low-heat setting for 8 to 10 hours. Place meat on serving platter; remove skewers or string. Slice into 4 equal pieces. Skim excess fat from soup mixture. Spoon some over meat; pass remaining. Makes 4 servings.

SWISS STEAK IN WINE SAUCE

1 2-pound beef round steak,
    cut 1 inch thick
2 tablespoons all-purpose flour
2 teaspoons salt
2 tablespoons cooking oil
1 cup chopped onion
½ cup sliced carrot

2 tablespoons chopped green
    pepper
1 16-ounce can tomatoes, cut up
¾ cup Burgundy
1 clove garlic, minced
1 teaspoon sugar
    Wine Sauce

Trim fat from steak; cut meat into 6 equal pieces. Coat with mixture of flour, salt, and ¼ teaspoon pepper. Pound steak to ½-inch thickness using meat mallet. Brown meat in hot oil; drain. Place onion, carrot, and green pepper in crockery cooker. Place meat atop. Combine undrained tomatoes, Burgundy, garlic, and sugar. Pour over meat. Cover; cook on low-heat setting for 8 to 10 hours. Transfer meat and vegetables to serving platter. Reserve 1½ cups of the cooking liquid for Wine Sauce. Spoon some sauce over meat; pass remaining sauce. Makes 6 servings.

Wine Sauce: Pour reserved liquid into saucepan. Blend ¼ cup cold water slowly into 2 tablespoons all-purpose flour; stir into liquid. Cook and stir till thickened and bubbly. Season to taste.

TEST KITCHEN TIP—A FULL POT

The heat in a coil-wrapped crockery cooker comes from the sides, so a cooker that is at least half full will be the most efficient. Since removing the meat may cause the remaining liquid to fall below the half-full mark, the liquid will often be easier to thicken if it is transferred to a saucepan.

BEEF BRISKET HUTSPOT

6 medium potatoes, peeled
    and chopped
6 medium carrots, sliced
3 medium onions, sliced
1 2½-pound boneless fresh
    beef brisket
1½ teaspoons salt

Dash paprika
1 bay leaf
2 tablespoons butter *or*
    margarine
3 tablespoons all-purpose flour
½ teaspoon beef-flavored gravy
    base

In crockery cooker place potatoes, carrots, and onions. Trim excess fat from brisket. Sprinkle with salt, paprika, and dash pepper; place atop vegetables. Add bay leaf and 1½ cups water. Cover; cook on low-heat setting for 12 to 14 hours. Remove bay leaf. Lift out brisket to cutting board. Drain vegetables; reserve 1½ cups cooking liquid. Add butter to vegetables; mash. Season with salt and pepper. Keep meat and vegetables warm; prepare gravy. In saucepan blend ½ cup cold water slowly into flour; stir in reserved cooking liquid and gravy base. Cook and stir till thickened and bubbly. Season to taste. Slice brisket thinly across grain. Serve with the vegetables and gravy. Serves 6.

CORNED BEEF IN BEER

6 medium potatoes, peeled
    and quartered
3 medium onions, peeled
    and quartered

1 cup thinly sliced carrots
1 3- to 4-pound corned beef
    brisket
1 cup beer

In crockery cooker place potatoes, onions, and carrots. Trim the excess fat from corned beef brisket; place meat atop vegetables. Pour beer over all. Cover and cook on low-heat setting for 9 to 11 hours. Slice the beef brisket thinly across the grain. Serve with vegetables. Makes 6 servings.

SPICY CIDER CORNED BEEF

3 medium onions, sliced
1 small head cabbage, cut
    in wedges
1 3- to 4-pound corned beef
    brisket
        • • •
1 cup apple cider

¼ cup packed brown sugar
2 teaspoons grated orange peel
2 teaspoons prepared mustard
6 whole cloves
1 14-ounce jar spiced apple
    rings

Place onions and cabbage in crockery cooker. Trim fat from brisket; place meat atop vegetables. Stir together cider, brown sugar, orange peel, mustard, and cloves; pour over meat. Cover; cook on low-heat setting for 8 to 10 hours. Garnish platter with apple rings. Pass mustard; if desired. Serves 6 to 8.

EASTERN BEEF AND EGGPLANT

1 small eggplant, peeled
  and cubed
1 8-ounce can tomato sauce
½ cup chopped celery
½ cup chopped onion
¼ cup chopped green pepper

½ teaspoon salt
¼ teaspoon dried marjoram,
  crushed
⅛ teaspoon ground cinnamon
⅛ teaspoon ground nutmeg
2 cups cubed cooked beef

In crockery cooker stir together the eggplant, tomato sauce, celery, onion, green pepper, salt, marjoram, cinnamon, and nutmeg. Cover; cook on low-heat setting for 8 to 10 hours. Turn cooker to high-heat setting; stir in cubed beef. Cover; heat through, 30 to 45 minutes. Makes 5 or 6 servings.

HUNGARIAN GOULASH

In plastic bag combine ⅓ cup all-purpose flour, 1 teaspoon salt, and dash pepper. Cut one 2 pound beef chuck pot roast into 1-inch cubes. Add to flour mixture; shake to coat. In skillet brown meat on all sides in 2 tablespoons hot cooking oil. Drain; transfer to crockery cooker. Stir in 1 cup water, ½ cup chopped onion, 2 tablespoons catsup, 2 teaspoons instant beef bouillon granules, 1 teaspoon paprika, and 2 bay leaves. Cover; cook on low-heat setting for 8 to 10 hours. Turn cooker to high-heat setting. When mixture boils remove bay leaves. Combine ½ cup dairy sour cream and 3 tablespoons all-purpose flour. Slowly blend 1 cup hot cooking liquid into sour cream; return to hot mixture. Cook and stir till thickened. Serve over hot cooked noodles. Serves 6.

LIMA-MEATBALL CASSEROLE

½ pound bulk pork sausage
1 beaten egg
½ cup fine dry bread crumbs
½ cup chopped onion
¼ cup chopped green pepper
½ teaspoon dried marjoram,
  crushed

½ teaspoon salt
1 pound ground beef
2 tablespoons all-purpose flour
2 16-ounce cans lima beans
½ teaspoon beef-flavored gravy
  base

In skillet cook sausage till lightly browned; drain. Transfer to crockery cooker. Combine egg, bread crumbs, onion, green pepper, marjoram, salt, and dash pepper. Add ground beef; mix well. Shape the mixture into 30 small meatballs. In same skillet brown meatballs on all sides; drain, reserving drippings. Stir flour into drippings. Drain lima beans; reserve liquid. Blend bean liquid slowly into flour mixture; add gravy base and dash pepper. Cook and stir till thickened and bubbly. Combine gravy and beans with sausage in cooker; add meatballs. Cover; cook on low-heat setting for 8 to 9 hours. Sprinkle chopped green pepper atop, if desired. Serves 6 to 8.

MEAT LOAF DINNER

6 potatoes, peeled and cubed
4 carrots, thinly sliced
● ● ●
1 slightly beaten egg
1 large shredded wheat biscuit,
  crushed (½ cup)
¼ cup chili sauce

¼ cup finely chopped onion
½ teaspoon salt
¼ teaspoon dried marjoram,
  crushed
⅛ teaspoon pepper
1 pound ground beef

In a crockery cooker place potatoes and carrots. Season lightly with salt. In a bowl combine egg, crushed shredded wheat biscuit, chili sauce, onion, ½ teaspoon salt, marjoram, and pepper. Add ground beef; mix well. Shape meat mixture into a round loaf slightly smaller in diameter than the cooker; place atop the vegetables, not touching sides of cooker. Cover and cook on low-heat setting for 9 to 10 hours. Remove meat loaf from cooker using two spatulas; drain off the excess fat.

Place meat loaf on warm serving platter; arrange potatoes and carrots around the loaf. Makes 4 servings.

CHILI LOAF

2 slightly beaten eggs
1 10-ounce can mild enchilada
  sauce
1 8-ounce can tomatoes, cut up
1 8-ounce can red kidney beans,
  drained
1 cup crushed corn chips
¼ cup finely chopped green
  onion with tops

2 tablespoons snipped parsley
1 teaspoon salt
1 teaspoon chili powder
1 pound ground beef
1 pound bulk pork sausage
● ● ●
½ cup shredded sharp American
  cheese (2 ounces)

In a bowl combine eggs, *2 tablespoons* of the enchilada sauce, undrained tomatoes, beans, corn chips, green onion, parsley, salt, and chili powder. Add ground beef and sausage; mix well. Shape meat mixture into a round loaf slightly smaller in diameter than a crockery cooker. Place the meat loaf on a rack in cooker so that sides do not touch cooker. Cover and cook on low-heat setting for 10 hours. In saucepan heat the remaining enchilada sauce. Pass sauce and cheese to top each serving. Makes 8 servings.

TEST KITCHEN TIP—HELP FOR MEAT LOAVES

For easiest removal of a cooked meat loaf, use two spatulas or make foil "handles." Cut two 15x2-inch strips of foil (use heavy-duty or a double thickness of regular). Crisscross the strips across the bottom and up the sides of the cooker *before* placing the shaped meat loaf inside.

TANGY MEAT LOAF

2 beaten eggs
1 8-ounce container onion
   sour cream dip
2¼ cups soft bread crumbs
½ cup finely chopped celery
¼ cup chopped onion
2 tablespoons chopped pimiento

1 teaspoon dried dillweed
¾ teaspoon salt
Dash pepper
• • •
1 pound ground beef
1 pound ground pork
Sour Cream-Mushroom Sauce

In a large bowl combine the eggs, ½ cup of the sour cream dip, the bread crumbs, celery, onion, pimiento, dillweed, salt, and pepper; mix well. Blend in the ground beef and pork. In crockery cooker crisscross two 15x2-inch strips of foil (use heavy-duty or double thickness of regular) across the bottom and up the sides. Place the meat mixture atop foil strips, pressing lightly to shape into a round loaf that doesn't touch the sides of the cooker. Cover; cook on low-heat setting for 8 to 9 hours. Lift out the meat loaf, using the foil "handles"; drain off excess fat. Serve with Sour Cream-Mushroom Sauce. Makes 8 servings.

Sour Cream-Mushroom Sauce: In saucepan combine remaining ½ cup onion sour cream dip and one 10¾-ounce can condensed cream of mushroom soup. Heat through; stir occasionally.

DUTCH-STYLE BEEF AND CABBAGE

1 1½-pound beef round steak,
   cut ¾ inch thick
2 tablespoons all-purpose flour
1 teaspoon salt
¼ teaspoon pepper
2 tablespoons cooking oil

3 large onions, sliced (3 cups)
¾ cup hot water
1 tablespoon vinegar
2 teaspoons instant beef
   bouillon granules
1 small head cabbage

Trim excess fat from meat; cut into cubes. Combine flour, salt, and pepper; coat meat with flour mixture. In skillet quickly brown meat on all sides in hot oil. Drain off fat. Transfer meat to crockery cooker; add onions. In same skillet combine water, vinegar, and bouillon granules. Stir together, scraping browned bits from skillet; pour all into cooker. Cover and cook on low-heat setting for 8 hours.

About 15 minutes before serving, cut cabbage into 4 or 5 wedges. Cook in a 3-quart saucepan in a large amount of boiling salted water till tender, 10 to 12 minutes. Drain well. Serve beef mixture over hot cooked cabbage wedges. Makes 4 or 5 servings.

Remember Dutch-Style Beef and Cabbage when you need a hearty main dish. Cubes of beef round steak slow-cook all day in a vinegar-seasoned beef broth. Serve with cooked cabbage wedges.

BEEF STEW BOURGUIGNONNE

2 pounds beef stew meat, cut
  in 1-inch cubes
2 tablespoons cooking oil
1 10¾-ounce can condensed
  golden mushroom soup
½ cup chopped onion
½ cup shredded carrot
⅓ cup dry red wine

1 3-ounce can chopped
  mushrooms, drained
¼ teaspoon dried oregano,
  crushed
¼ teaspoon Worcestershire
  sauce
¼ cup all-purpose flour
  Hot cooked noodles

In skillet brown meat in hot oil; drain. Transfer meat to crockery cooker. Stir in soup, onion, carrot, wine, mushrooms, oregano, and Worcestershire. Cover; cook on low-heat setting for 10 to 12 hours. Turn cooker to high-heat setting. Blend ½ cup cold water slowly into flour; stir into beef mixture. Cook and stir till thickened and bubbly. Serve beef mixture over noodles. Serves 6.

SIMMERED BEEF SHANKS

In plastic bag combine 3 tablespoons all-purpose flour, 1 teaspoon salt, and ¼ teaspoon pepper. Add 4 pounds beef shank cross cuts, one shank at a time; shake to coat. In skillet brown meat in 2 tablespoons hot cooking oil. In crockery cooker place 3 cups chopped potatoes; place meat atop. Stir together 1 cup water; one 6-ounce can tomato paste; 1 teaspoon dried basil, crushed; and ½ teaspoon salt. Pour over meat. Cover; cook on low-heat setting for 9 to 10 hours. Remove meat and potatoes to serving dish. Sprinkle with 2 tablespoons snipped parsley; cover to keep warm. Skim fat from cooking liquid; measure 1½ cups into saucepan. Blend 2 tablespoons cold water slowly into 1 tablespoon cornstarch; stir into liquid. Cook and stir till thickened and bubbly; season to taste. Serve with meat and potatoes. Makes 4 servings.

TURKEY CHABLIS

1 28-ounce frozen rolled turkey
  roast, thawed
¾ cup dry white wine
½ cup finely chopped onion
1 clove garlic, minced

1 bay leaf
¼ teaspoon dried rosemary,
  crushed
⅓ cup light cream or milk
2 tablespoons cornstarch

Place thawed turkey roast in crockery cooker. Combine wine, onion, garlic, bay leaf, rosemary, and ⅛ teaspoon pepper; pour over turkey. Cover; cook on low-heat setting for 9 hours. Remove roast; keep warm. Discard bay leaf. Skim excess fat from cooking liquid; measure 1⅓ cups cooking liquid into saucepan. Blend cream slowly into cornstarch; stir into liquid. Cook and stir till thickened and bubbly. Season to taste. Slice roast. Spoon some sauce over; pass remaining. Garnish with parsley, if desired. Serves 4 to 6.

TURKEY ROSEMARY

Ask your meatman to cut the turkey hindquarters in halves or thirds—

4 pounds frozen turkey
  hindquarters, thawed
2 tablespoons cooking oil
  • • •
2 medium onions, coarsely
  chopped (1 cup)
2 large stalks celery, coarsely
  chopped (1 cup)

2 teaspoons instant chicken
  bouillon granules
1 teaspoon dried rosemary,
  crushed
½ teaspoon salt
  Dash pepper
¼ cup all-purpose flour

In skillet brown turkey pieces in hot oil; drain off excess fat. In crockery cooker combine onion, celery, bouillon granules, rosemary, salt, pepper, and 1 cup water. Place turkey pieces atop. Cover; cook on low-heat setting for 8 hours. Remove turkey pieces. Skim excess fat from cooking liquid; measure 1½ cups liquid into saucepan. Return turkey pieces to cooker; cover. Blend ½ cup cold water slowly into flour; stir into reserved cooking liquid in saucepan. Cook and stir till gravy is thickened and bubbly; season to taste. Place turkey pieces on serving platter; pass the gravy. Makes 6 servings.

SWISS ONION AND CHICKEN

2 cups sliced onions
2 tablespoons butter *or*
  margarine
8 slices day-old bread, cubed
  (8 cups)
2 cups chopped cooked chicken

1½ cups shredded Swiss cheese
  (6 ounces)
4 eggs
2 cups milk
1 teaspoon salt
2 tablespoons snipped parsley

In skillet cook onion in butter till tender. Place ⅓ of the bread cubes in a greased 2-pound coffee can *or* 3-pound shortening can. Add *half* the onions, chicken, and cheese. Repeat layers ending with bread cubes. Press lightly, if necessary, to fit. Beat eggs, milk, and salt together; pour over bread. Cover with foil, crimping edges to sides of can; set in crockery cooker. Pour ½ cup water into cooker. Cover; cook on low-heat setting for 8 to 9 hours. Remove from cooker; let stand 5 to 10 minutes. Loosen edges with spatula or knife. Carefully turn into a serving bowl. Garnish with snipped parsley. Makes 6 to 8 servings.

TEST KITCHEN TIP—USING A TIMER

Plug your crockery cooker into an automatic timer to start the cooking while you're away from home. Just before you leave, place chilled food in the cooker; cover. Set the timer to turn on the cooker at a specific time, making sure the uncooked foods stand no more than 2 hours before the cooker comes on.

Try *Chicken and Sausage Cassoulet* for a meal-in-one-dish
combination that is spiced to perfection. Dried beans plus
chopped carrot, onion, and celery enhance the hearty full flavor.

CHICKEN AND SAUSAGE CASSOULET

1¼ cups dry navy beans
½ pound bulk pork sausage
1 2½- to 3-pound ready-to-cook
   broiler-fryer chicken,
   cut up
½ cup finely chopped carrot
½ cup chopped celery
½ cup chopped onion
1½ cups tomato juice

1 tablespoon Worcestershire
   sauce
2 teaspoons instant beef
   bouillon granules
1 teaspoon salt
½ teaspoon dried basil, crushed
½ teaspoon dried oregano,
   crushed
½ teaspoon paprika

Advance preparation: In large saucepan bring beans and 4 cups water to
boiling. Reduce heat and simmer, covered, for 1½ hours. Pour beans and
liquid into bowl. Refrigerate overnight.

Shape sausage into 18 balls; brown
in skillet. Remove meatballs; reserve
drippings in skillet. Cover meatballs;
refrigerate overnight. Sprinkle chicken
with salt and pepper; brown in the

reserved drippings. Remove chicken;
cover and refrigerate overnight.
Before serving: In crockery cooker
place chicken, meatballs, carrot, celery,
and onion. Drain beans; mix with remaining ingredients. Pour over meat
mixture. Cover; cook on low-heat setting for 8 hours. Remove chicken and
meatballs. Mash bean mixture slightly;
serve with meat. Makes 6 servings.

CROCKERY-STEWED CHICKEN

1 4-pound ready-to-cook
    stewing chicken, cut up
4 celery stalks with leaves,
    cut up
4 cups water
1 small onion, sliced
2 sprigs parsley

1 bay leaf
1 teaspoon salt
¼ teaspoon pepper
¼ teaspoon dried thyme, crushed
¼ teaspoon dried marjoram,
    crushed
¼ teaspoon celery salt

In crockery cooker combine all ingredients. Cover and cook on low-heat setting for 8 to 10 hours. Remove chicken from cooker. Strain chicken broth; store in covered container. Chill. As soon as chicken is cool enough to handle; remove meat from bones. Discard bones and skin. Place chicken in covered container; refrigerate. Makes 4 cups cooked chicken and 4 cups chicken broth.

CHICKEN WITH ARTICHOKES

Skin, split, and bone 4 medium chicken breasts (2½ pounds). In skillet brown chicken on all sides in 1 tablespoon hot cooking oil; drain. Transfer to crockery cooker. Stir together one 8-ounce can tomato sauce; ½ cup dry sherry; 1 envelope spaghetti sauce mix; and one 3-ounce can sliced mushrooms, drained. Pour over chicken. Cover and cook on low-heat setting for 8 to 9 hours.

Remove chicken to platter; cover. Pour tomato mixture into saucepan. Stir in one 9-ounce package frozen artichoke hearts, thawed; cover and bring to boiling. Blend 1 tablespoon cold water slowly into 2 teaspoons cornstarch; stir into sauce. Cook and stir till mixture is thickened and bubbly. Spoon some sauce over chicken; pass the remaining. Makes 4 servings.

CHICKEN AND SPAGHETTI

4 small chicken breasts,
    split, skinned, and boned
2 tablespoons cooking oil
1 8-ounce can tomato sauce
1 6-ounce can tomato paste
¼ cup water
3 cloves garlic, minced

2 teaspoons dried oregano,
    crushed
1 teaspoon sugar
1 4-ounce package shredded
    mozzarella cheese (1 cup)
    Hot cooked spaghetti
    Grated Parmesan cheese

In skillet brown the chicken in hot oil; drain. Sprinkle generously with salt and pepper. Transfer to crockery cooker. Combine tomato sauce, tomato paste, water, garlic, oregano, and sugar. Pour sauce over chicken. Cover and cook on low-heat setting for 8 to 9 hours. Remove chicken and keep warm. Turn cooker to high-heat setting; stir mozzarella cheese into sauce. Cook, covered, till cheese melts and sauce is heated through. Serve chicken and sauce over cooked spaghetti. Pass Parmesan. Makes 4 servings.

PORK CHOPS IN BREW

Trim fat from 6 pork chops, cut ¾ inch thick; cook trimmings in skillet till 1 tablespoon fat accumulates. Discard trimmings. Brown chops on both sides in hot fat; season with salt and pepper. Thinly slice 2 medium onions; place in crockery cooker. Arrange chops atop. Dissolve 1 teaspoon instant chicken bouillon granules in one 12-ounce can dark *or* light beer (1½ cups). Stir in ¼ teaspoon dried thyme, crushed; pour over chops. Cover; cook on low-heat setting for 8 to 10 hours. Arrange chops and onions on warm platter over hot cooked noodles *or* mashed potatoes.

Skim fat from cooking liquid; serve with chops. If thicker gravy is desired, measure 1½ cups hot liquid into saucepan. Blend ⅓ cup cold water slowly into 3 tablespoons all-purpose flour; stir into hot liquid. Add ½ teaspoon Kitchen Bouquet, if desired. Cook and stir till thickened and bubbly. Season to taste with salt and pepper. Serves 6.

CHINESE PORK ROAST

1 3- to 4-pound pork shoulder
   roast
1 teaspoon salt
2½ teaspoons curry powder
2 tablespoons cooking oil
1 10¾-ounce can condensed
   cream of mushroom soup

1 16-ounce can fancy mixed
   Chinese vegetables, drained
2 cups cooked rice
¼ cup cold water
2 tablespoons all-purpose flour
   Soy sauce

Trim excess fat from roast; cut to fit into crockery cooker. Combine salt and ½ *teaspoon* of the curry powder; rub into roast. Brown roast on all sides in hot oil. Place roast on rack in cooker. Combine mushroom soup and remaining 2 teaspoons curry powder; pour over meat. Cover; cook on low-heat setting for 8 to 10 hours. Turn cooker to high-heat setting; bring to boiling, about 10 minutes. Remove roast to platter. Stir Chinese vegetables and rice into sauce. Blend cold water slowly into flour; stir into sauce. Cook and stir till thickened; serve with roast. Pass soy. Makes 8 servings.

CRANBERRY-WINE SAUCED PORK

Cut one 2-pound boneless smoked pork shoulder in half, if necessary, to fit in a crockery cooker. Combine one 8-ounce can whole cranberry sauce, ⅓ cup sugar, ¼ cup dry red wine, 1 teaspoon prepared mustard, and ⅛ teaspoon ground cloves; pour over pork. Cover and cook on low-heat setting for 8 to 10 hours. Remove meat to platter; keep warm. Skim the excess fat from cranberry mixture; measure 2 cups liquid, adding water if necessary.

In saucepan blend 2 tablespoons cold water slowly into 2 tablespoons cornstarch. Gradually stir in the hot cranberry mixture. Cook and stir till thickened and bubbly, about 5 minutes. Slice pork. Spoon some of the hot cranberry sauce over the slices; pass the remaining. Makes 6 to 8 servings.

PEACHY PORK STEAKS

4 pork steaks, cut ½ inch thick
    (about 1½ pounds)
¾ teaspoon dried basil,
    crushed
¼ teaspoon salt
    Dash pepper
1 16-ounce can peach slices

2 tablespoons vinegar
1 tablespoon instant beef
    bouillon granules
    Hot cooked rice
¼ cup cold water
2 tablespoons cornstarch

Trim fat from steaks. In skillet cook trimmings till about 2 tablespoons fat accumulate; discard trimmings. Brown steaks on both sides in hot fat. Sprinkle with basil, salt, and pepper. Drain peach slices; reserve syrup. Place peaches in crockery cooker; place meat atop. Combine reserved peach syrup, vinegar, and bouillon granules; pour over steaks. Cover; cook on low-heat setting for 8 hours. Arrange steaks and peaches atop rice on platter; keep warm. Garnish with parsley, if desired. Skim excess fat from cooking liquid. In saucepan blend cold water into cornstarch; stir in the hot liquid. Cook and stir till thickened and bubbly. Serve with steaks. Makes 4 servings.

SMOKED PORK AND KRAUT

2 medium onions, cut into
    wedges
1 2-pound boneless smoked
    pork shoulder
1 27-ounce can sauerkraut,
    rinsed and drained
1 8-ounce can tomatoes,
    cut up

1 bay leaf
1 tablespoon paprika
1½ teaspoons caraway seed
¼ teaspoon pepper
¼ cup cold water
2 tablespoons cornstarch
½ cup dairy sour cream

Place onion in crockery cooker. Place pork atop. Combine sauerkraut, undrained tomatoes, bay leaf, paprika, caraway seed, and pepper; pour over pork. Cover; cook on low-heat setting for 8 hours. Remove bay leaf. Transfer pork to serving platter; cover to keep warm. Skim fat from surface of sauerkraut mixture, if necessary; pour into large saucepan. Blend cold water into cornstarch; stir into sauerkraut. Cook and stir till thickened and bubbly. Stir in sour cream. Sprinkle with paprika, if desired; serve with pork. Serves 6.

TEST KITCHEN TIP—GARNISHES

Brighten your crockery meals with an attractive garnish. On soups and stews sprinkle crushed corn chips, snipped parsley, or shredded cheese. Trim other main dishes with orange or lemon slices, carrot curls, bacon curls, cherry tomatoes, radish roses, or pimiento-stuffed green olives.

PORK MARENGO

**2 pounds boneless pork shoulder,
  cut in 1-inch cubes**
½ cup chopped onion
2 tablespoons cooking oil
1 16-ounce can tomatoes, cut up
**1 teaspoon instant chicken
  bouillon granules**
**1 teaspoon dried marjoram,
  crushed**

1 teaspoon salt
**½ teaspoon dried thyme, crushed
  Dash pepper**
• • •
**1 3-ounce can chopped mushrooms,
  drained**
⅓ cup cold water
**3 tablespoons all-purpose flour
  Hot cooked rice**

In skillet brown *half* of the pork cubes and chopped onion at a time in hot oil; drain off fat. Transfer meat and onion to crockery cooker. In same skillet combine undrained tomatoes, bouillon granules, marjoram, salt, thyme, and pepper. Stir together, scraping browned bits from bottom of skillet; pour over pork. Cover; cook on low-heat setting for 8 to 10 hours. Turn to high-heat setting. Stir in drained mushrooms. Blend cold water slowly into flour; stir into pork mixture. Cook, uncovered, on high-heat setting till thickened, 15 to 20 minutes; stir occasionally. Serve over rice. Makes 6 to 8 servings.

PORK STROGANOFF

**1½ pounds boneless pork
  shoulder, cut in
  ¾-inch cubes**
1 tablespoon cooking oil
½ cup chopped onion
1 clove garlic, minced
1 cup water
**1 3-ounce can chopped
  mushrooms, drained**

**1 tablespoon instant beef
  bouillon granules**
1 teaspoon dried dillweed
⅛ teaspoon pepper
• • •
½ cup dairy sour cream
¼ cup dry white wine
**3 tablespoons all-purpose flour
  Hot cooked noodles**

In skillet brown the pork cubes on all sides in hot oil; drain. Add the onion and garlic; cook till tender but not brown. Transfer meat mixture to crockery cooker. Combine the water, mushrooms, bouillon granules, dillweed, and pepper; pour over meat. Cover and cook on low-heat setting for 8 to 10 hours. Turn to high-heat setting. Heat till bubbly, 15 to 20 minutes. Blend together the sour cream, wine, and flour. Stir into the hot mixture; heat through, about 15 minutes, stirring occasionally. Serve over noodles. Sprinkle with snipped parsley, if desired. Makes 6 servings.

Pork Marengo features cubed pork in an herbed tomato sauce for a
flavorful meat-stretching dish friends will enjoy. If you are
cooking for only two, freeze the extra portions for another day.

CURRIED PORK DINNER

2 pounds boneless pork
   shoulder, cut in
   ¾-inch cubes
2 tablespoons cooking oil
½ teaspoon salt
⅛ teaspoon pepper
1 cup chopped onion
1 cup diced apple

3 tablespoons curry powder
½ teaspoon paprika
½ teaspoon dried oregano,
   crushed
2 teaspoons instant chicken
   bouillon granules
1 tablespoon all-purpose flour
   Hot cooked rice

In skillet brown pork in hot oil. Transfer to crockery cooker; sprinkle with salt and pepper. Add onion, apple, curry, paprika, and oregano. Mix bouillon and 1 cup hot water; pour over pork mixture. Cover; cook on low-heat setting for 8 to 10 hours. Turn to high-heat setting. Blend 2 tablespoons cold water into flour; stir into pork mixture. Cover; cook till thickened, about 15 minutes. Serve over rice; garnish with apple wedges, if desired. Serves 6 to 8.

HAM HOCKS AND BLACK-EYED PEAS

In saucepan bring 6 cups water and 1½ cups dry black-eyed peas to boiling; reduce heat. Simmer, covered, for 1½ hours. Pour peas and liquid into bowl. Cover; refrigerate overnight.

Drain beans; reserve liquid. Add water to make 1 cup. In crockery cooker combine beans and liquid, 4 small smoked ham hocks (1½ pounds), ½ cup chopped onion, ½ cup chopped celery, 2 bay leaves, and ⅛ teaspoon cayenne. Cover; cook on low-heat setting for 10 to 12 hours. Turn to high-heat setting. Stir in ½ of a 10-ounce package frozen cut okra (¾ cup), partially thawed. Cover; cook till okra is tender, about 30 minutes. Remove bay leaves. Season to taste. Makes 6 servings.

HEARTY HODGEPODGE

6 slices bacon
1 cup chopped carrot
½ cup chopped onion
2 cups diced potatoes
1 15-ounce can garbanzo
   beans, undrained

1 pound beef shank cross cuts
1 ¾-pound ham hock
1 clove garlic, minced
2 teaspoons salt
1 4-ounce link Polish
   sausage, thinly sliced

In skillet cook bacon till crisp; drain, reserving 2 tablespoons drippings. Crumble bacon; wrap and chill. Cook carrot and onion in drippings till tender but not brown. In crockery cooker combine potatoes, garbanzo beans, carrot, and onion. Add beef, ham hock, garlic, salt, and 4 cups water. Cover; cook on low-heat setting for 10 to 12 hours. Turn cooker to high-heat setting. Remove beef shank and ham hock. Cut meat from bones; return meat to cooker. Stir in sausage and bacon. Cover; cook 30 to 40 minutes. Skim fat. Serves 8 to 10.

LAMB PAPRIKASH

2 pounds lean lamb, cut in
    1-inch pieces
1 16-ounce can tomatoes, cut up
1 cup chopped onion
1 clove garlic, minced
1 teaspoon salt
1 teaspoon paprika
½ cup cold water
¼ cup all-purpose flour
½ cup dairy sour cream
    Hot cooked noodles
    Snipped parsley

In crockery cooker combine lamb, undrained tomatoes, onion, garlic, salt, and paprika. Cover and cook on low-heat setting for 8 to 10 hours. Turn cooker to high-heat setting; spoon off the excess fat. Blend cold water slowly into flour; stir into the meat mixture. Cover; cook till thickened and bubbly, 20 to 30 minutes. Stir mixture occasionally. Blend about ½ cup of the hot mixture into sour cream; stir into remaining mixture in cooker. Heat through. Serve over noodles; garnish with parsley. Makes 6 servings.

MANDARIN LAMB SHANKS

6 lamb shanks, halved
    crosswise (4 pounds)
1 10½-ounce can condensed
    beef broth
2 tablespoons lemon juice
1 tablespoon anchovy paste
    (optional)
1 teaspoon dried oregano,
    crushed
½ teaspoon dry mustard
¼ teaspoon garlic powder
¾ cup cold water
2 tablespoons all-purpose flour
1 11-ounce can mandarin orange
    sections, drained
½ teaspoon Kitchen Bouquet
    (optional)
    Hot cooked rice

Place lamb in large plastic bag set in deep bowl. Combine broth, lemon juice, anchovy paste, oregano, mustard, and garlic powder. Pour over lamb in bag and close; refrigerate overnight, turning bag twice to coat meat. Drain meat, reserving marinade. Measure; add water if necessary to make 1½ cups. Place lamb shanks in crockery cooker. Add *1 cup* of the reserved marinade; chill remaining marinade. Cover cooker; cook on low-heat setting for 8 to 10 hours. Discard cooking liquid. Return meat to cooker to keep warm. In saucepan blend cold water slowly into flour; add remaining marinade. Cook and stir till thickened. Stir in oranges and Kitchen Bouquet; heat through. Season to taste. Serve lamb and sauce over rice. Serves 6.

TEST KITCHEN TIP—TO REDUCE COOKING TIME

Most foods cook on the high-heat setting in half the time they require on the low-heat setting. So, if a recipe calls for 10 hours on low, you can turn the cooker to high and allow 5 hours for the food to cook.

HERBED BEEF AND TOMATOES

1 medium onion, thinly sliced	½ teaspoon salt
1 2-pound beef round steak, cut ¾ inch thick	⅛ teaspoon paprika
2 tablespoons cooking oil	⅛ teaspoon pepper
1 cup beef broth *or* Beef Stock (see recipe, page 43)	2 tablespoons cold water
1 clove garlic, minced	1 tablespoon soy sauce
1 teaspoon Worcestershire sauce	3 tablespoons cornstarch
½ teaspoon dried rosemary, crushed	3 medium tomatoes, peeled and cut in wedges
	Hot cooked noodles
	Snipped parsley

Separate onion into rings; place in crockery cooker. Trim fat from meat; cut meat in 2x½-inch strips. In skillet brown meat in hot oil; drain. Stir into cooker with broth, garlic, Worcestershire, rosemary, salt, paprika, and pepper. Cover; cook on low-heat setting for 8 to 10 hours. Turn to high-heat setting. Skim off fat. Blend water and soy sauce into cornstarch; stir into hot mixture. Cover; cook till bubbly, 15 to 20 minutes. Stir in tomatoes; heat 5 minutes. Serve over noodles; top with parsley. Serves 6.

Herbed Beef and Tomatoes has an especially good flavor when made with homemade *Beef Stock* (see recipe, page 43). The stock also makes an excellent appetizer soup topped with sliced mushrooms.

KIDNEY IN WINE SAUCE

1 pound beef kidney
1 10½-ounce can condensed
   beef broth
½ cup thinly sliced carrot
½ cup sliced celery
½ cup chopped onion

1 small clove garlic, minced
¼ teaspoon salt

• • •

¼ cup dry red wine
2 tablespoons cornstarch
Hot cooked noodles

Split kidney lengthwise. Remove membranes and hard parts; cut meat in ½-inch strips. In crockery cooker place meat, beef broth, carrot, celery, onion, garlic, and salt. Cover; cook on low-heat setting for 10 to 12 hours. Turn to high-heat setting; bring to boiling. Blend wine into cornstarch; stir into kidney mixture. Cook and stir till thickened. Serve over noodles. Serves 4.

MARINATED BEEF HEART SLICES

Trim one 2-pound beef heart, removing skin, fat, and hard parts. Cut meat into ¼-inch-thick slices; place in plastic bag in deep bowl. Add ⅓ cup finely chopped onion; ¼ cup vinegar; ¼ cup sherry; 2 tablespoons cooking oil; 1 clove garlic, minced; 1 bay leaf; ½ teaspoon salt; ¼ teaspoon pepper; and few drops bottled hot pepper sauce. Close bag; turn over to distribute marinade. Refrigerate overnight. In crockery cooker place 2 medium carrots, shredded. Add meat, marinade, and ¼ cup water. Cover; cook on low-heat setting for 8 to 10 hours. Turn to high-heat setting. Blend ½ cup cold water slowly into ⅓ cup all-purpose flour; stir into hot mixture. Cover; cook till thickened and bubbly, about 20 minutes. Season to taste with salt and pepper. Serve the heart slices over hot cooked noodles. Makes 6 to 8 servings.

CHINESE STYLE BEEF TONGUE

4 medium potatoes, peeled and
   quartered
1 2- to 3-pound beef tongue
¼ cup soy sauce
1 tablespoon sherry
1 clove garlic, minced

2 teaspoons sugar
½ teaspoon salt
¼ teaspoon dried tarragon,
   crushed
¼ teaspoon ground ginger
2 tablespoons cornstarch

Place potatoes and tongue in crockery cooker. Add soy, sherry, garlic, sugar, salt, tarragon, ginger, and 1 cup water. Cover; cook on low-heat setting for 8 hours. Turn to high-heat setting. Remove tongue; cut bones and gristle from large end. Split skin on underside from large end to tip; peel off. Slice tongue on a slant. Arrange on platter with potatoes; keep warm. Skim fat from broth. Measure 2 cups broth; return to cooker. Blend 2 tablespoons cold water slowly into cornstarch. Stir into broth. Cook and stir till thickened. Pour some gravy over meat; pass remaining. Serves 6 to 8.

34 *spaghetti sauces*

SPAGHETTI WITH MEAT SAUCE

1 pound ground beef
2 28-ounce cans tomatoes
2 medium onions, quartered
2 medium carrots, cut
   in chunks
2 cloves garlic, minced
1 6-ounce can tomato paste
2 tablespoons snipped parsley
1 bay leaf
1 tablespoon sugar

1 teaspoon dried basil,
   crushed
¾ teaspoon salt
½ teaspoon dried oregano,
   crushed
Dash pepper
2 tablespoons cold water
2 tablespoons cornstarch
Hot cooked spaghetti
Grated Parmesan cheese

In skillet brown the ground beef; drain off excess fat. Transfer meat to a crockery cooker. In blender container place *one* can of tomatoes, undrained. Add the onion, carrot, and garlic. Cover and blend till chopped; stir into meat in cooker. Cut up the remaining can of tomatoes but do not drain; stir into meat mixture with tomato paste, parsley, bay leaf, sugar, basil, salt, oregano, and pepper. Mix well. Cover and cook on low-heat setting for 8 to 10 hours. To serve, turn to high-heat setting. Remove bay leaf. Cover and heat till bubbly, 10 minutes. Blend cold water slowly into cornstarch; stir into tomato mixture. Cover and cook 10 minutes longer. Spoon over the spaghetti. Pass the Parmesan cheese to sprinkle atop. Makes 8 servings.

ANCHOVY-TOMATO SPAGHETTI SAUCE

1 28-ounce can tomatoes,
   cut up
1 15-ounce can tomato sauce
1 cup finely chopped onion
¼ cup chopped green pepper
1 2-ounce can anchovy fillets,
   drained and chopped
2 cloves garlic, minced
1 large bay leaf
1 tablespoon sugar
1½ teaspoons dried basil,
   crushed

1 teaspoon dried oregano,
   crushed
1 teaspoon salt
¼ teaspoon pepper
   • • •
1 tablespoon cold water
1 tablespoon cornstarch
Fine dry bread crumbs
   or grated Parmesan
   cheese
Hot cooked spaghetti

In crockery cooker combine undrained tomatoes, tomato sauce, onion, green pepper, anchovies, garlic, bay leaf, sugar, basil, oregano, salt, and pepper. Cover and cook on low-heat setting for 8 to 10 hours. To serve, turn cooker to high-heat setting. Remove bay leaf. Blend cold water slowly into cornstarch; stir into spaghetti sauce. Cover; cook till thickened and bubbly. If desired, in skillet carefully brown bread crumbs over low heat without butter or shortening; place in bowl. Spoon spaghetti sauce over hot spaghetti. Pass bread crumbs or Parmesan to sprinkle atop. Makes 6 servings.

SAUSAGE CHILI

1 pound bulk pork sausage
1 pound ground beef
● ● ●
2 15½-ounce cans red-kidney
   beans, drained
1 28-ounce can tomatoes,
   cut up

1 cup chopped onion
1 cup chopped green pepper
1 cup sliced celery
1 6-ounce can tomato paste
2 cloves garlic, minced
2 teaspoons salt
2 teaspoons chili powder

In skillet cook sausage and ground beef till browned; drain off excess fat. Transfer meat to crockery cooker. Stir in the remaining ingredients. Cover and cook on the low-heat setting for 8 to 10 hours. Serves 10 to 12.

MEXICAN CHILI

2 15½-ounce cans red kidney
   beans, drained
1 28-ounce can tomatoes, cut up
1½ cups chopped celery
1 cup chopped onion
1 6-ounce can tomato paste
½ cup chopped green pepper
1 4-ounce can green chili
   peppers, drained, seeded,
   and chopped

2 tablespoons sugar
1 bay leaf
1 teaspoon salt
1 teaspoon dried marjoram,
   crushed
½ teaspoon garlic powder
   Dash pepper

1 pound ground beef

In crockery cooker combine kidney beans, undrained tomatoes, celery, onion, tomato paste, green pepper, green chilies, sugar, bay leaf, salt, marjoram, garlic powder, and pepper. In skillet brown ground beef; drain and stir into tomato mixture. Cover; cook on low-heat setting for 8 to 10 hours. Skim off excess fat. Remove bay leaf; stir before serving. Serves 10 to 12.

VEGETABLE-BEEF CHILI

1 pound ground beef
1 cup chopped onion
2 10-ounce packages frozen
   mixed vegetables
1 16-ounce can tomatoes, cut up

1 8-ounce can tomato sauce
½ cup water
1 tablespoon chili powder
1 teaspoon salt
1 teaspoon sugar

In skillet cook beef and onion till beef is browned; drain off excess fat. Transfer meat mixture to crockery cooker. Place frozen vegetables in strainer; rinse with hot water to separate. Stir vegetables, undrained tomatoes, tomato sauce, water, chili powder, salt, and sugar into beef mixture. Cover the cooker; cook on low-heat setting for 8 to 10 hours. Makes 4 servings.

SAVORY BEEF-VEGETABLE SOUP

All-day cooking develops the flavor of this hearty soup, shown on page 6—

1 cup chopped potato
1 cup chopped onion
1 cup chopped carrot
1 cup chopped celery
2 pounds beef shank
    cross cuts
1 tablespoon salt

Dash pepper
3 cups water
2 teaspoons beef-flavored gravy
    base
1 15½-ounce can cut green beans
1 16-ounce can whole kernel
    corn

In crockery cooker combine potato, onion, carrot, and celery. Place beef atop. Sprinkle with salt and pepper. Stir together water and gravy base; pour over beef. Cover and cook on low-heat setting for 10 to 12 hours. Turn to high-heat setting. Remove beef; skim off fat.

Stir in the undrained green beans and undrained corn. Cover and cook 30 minutes longer. Meanwhile, remove meat from bones; chop and return to soup. Season to taste. Cover and cook 5 minutes more. Stir soup before serving. Makes 10 to 12 servings.

CIDER STEW

2 pounds beef stew meat,
    cut in 1-inch cubes
3 tablespoons cooking oil
3 tablespoons all-purpose flour
2 teaspoons salt
¼ teaspoon dried thyme,
    crushed
¼ teaspoon pepper
4 carrots, chopped

3 potatoes, peeled and chopped
    (2½ cups)
2 onions, sliced
1 stalk celery, chopped
1 apple, chopped
2 cups apple cider
1 tablespoon vinegar
½ cup cold water
¼ cup all-purpose flour

In skillet or large saucepan brown half the meat at a time in hot oil. Drain off fat. Combine 3 tablespoons flour, salt, thyme, and pepper. Toss with browned meat to coat. Place carrots, potatoes, onion, celery, and apple in crockery cooker. Place meat atop. Combine apple cider and vinegar. Pour over meat. Cover; cook on low-heat setting for 10 to 12 hours. Turn cooker to high-heat setting. Blend cold water into ¼ cup flour; stir into stew. Cover; cook till thickened, about 15 minutes. Season to taste. Serves 8.

TEST KITCHEN TIP—KEEP YOUR COOKER COVERED

When you lift the cover of your slow cooker to stir, be sure to replace it immediately, especially on the low-heat setting. If you leave the pot uncovered, it can lose as much as 20° of important cooking heat in only 2 minutes. A *quick* peek will cool the food only 1 or 2 degrees.

PINTOS CON CARNE

In saucepan combine 3½ cups water, 1 cup dry pinto beans, and ½ teaspoon salt; bring to boiling. Reduce heat; simmer, covered, for 1½ hours. Pour beans and cooking liquid into bowl. Cover; refrigerate overnight.

In skillet brown 1 pound ground beef; drain and place in crockery cooker.

Stir in beans and liquid, one 15-ounce can tomato sauce, ½ cup chopped onion, and 1 tablespoon chili powder. Cover; cook on low-heat setting for 8 to 10 hours. Stir before serving. Pass shredded sharp American cheese to sprinkle atop each serving. Serve with corn chips, if desired. Makes 6 servings.

PHILADELPHIA PEPPER POT SOUP

If the veal knuckle has little meat, add 1 or 2 veal shoulder chops for richer flavor—

- **2 pounds honeycomb tripe**
  Salt
- **3 medium carrots, sliced**
- **1 large onion, sliced**
- **½ cup thinly sliced celery**
- **4 whole cloves**
- **2 bay leaves**
- **2 tablespoons snipped parsley**
- **1 teaspoon dried marjoram,**
  crushed

- **1 teaspoon dried savory,**
  crushed
- **1 teaspoon dried basil, crushed**
- **1 teaspoon salt**
- **1 teaspoon whole black pepper**
- **½ teaspoon dried thyme, crushed**
- **¼ to ½ teaspoon cayenne**
- **1 1½-pound veal knuckle**
- **1 15- or 16-ounce can sliced**
  potatoes, drained

In crockery cooker cover tripe with water; add 1 teaspoon salt for each quart of water used. Cover and cook on high-heat setting till tripe has a clear jelly-like appearance, 6 to 8 hours (or on low-heat setting for 16 to 18 hours). Drain and chill.

In cooker combine carrots, onion, celery, cloves, bay leaves, parsley, marjoram, savory, basil, salt, pepper, thyme, cayenne, and 4 cups water. Add

veal knuckle. Cover; cook on low-heat setting 10 to 12 hours. Turn cooker to high-heat setting. Remove meat and vegetables. Skim fat from broth. Cut meat from bone; return meat to broth. Discard bone and vegetables. Cut chilled, cooked tripe into ½-inch pieces; stir into broth with potatoes. Cover; cook on high-heat setting for 1 hour. Season to taste. Remove whole cloves and bay leaves. Serves 6.

PUERTO RICAN OXTAIL SOUP

In a skillet brown 2 pounds beef oxtails in 1 tablespoon hot cooking oil. Drain; place in crockery cooker. Stir in 1½ cups peeled and chopped pumpkin *or* yellow winter squash; 1½ cups water; one 8-ounce can cream-style corn; one 8-ounce can tomato sauce; ¾ cup

chopped onion; ½ cup chopped green pepper; ¼ cup snipped parsley; 1 clove garlic, minced; 2 teaspoons salt; and ⅛ teaspoon pepper. Cover; cook on low-heat setting for 12 to 14 hours. If desired, before serving stir in 1 cup hot cooked vermicelli. Makes 4 to 6 servings.

BEEF STEW WITH CORN BREAD

½ cup all-purpose flour
2 pounds beef stew meat, cut in
   1-inch pieces
3 tablespoons shortening
5 medium carrots, chopped
1 16-ounce can tomatoes, cut up
1 15½-ounce can cut green
   beans, drained

1 10-ounce package frozen
   Mexican-style vegetables
½ cup chopped onion
¼ cup chopped celery
¼ cup chili sauce *or* catsup
1 tablespoon instant beef
   bouillon granules
Golden Corn Bread

In plastic bag combine ¼ *cup* of the flour, ½ teaspoon salt, and ⅛ teaspoon pepper. Add beef cubes, a few at a time, shaking to coat. In skillet brown meat quickly in hot shortening; transfer to crockery cooker. Add carrots, undrained tomatoes, beans, Mexican-style vegetables, onion, celery, chili sauce, and bouillon granules; mix well. Cover; cook on low-heat setting for 8 to 10 hours. Blend ½ cup cold water slowly into remaining flour; stir into stew.

Cover; cook on high-heat setting till thickened, 30 minutes. Serve over Golden Corn Bread. Serves 8 or 9.
   Golden Corn Bread: Combine 1 cup all-purpose flour, 1 cup yellow cornmeal, ¼ cup sugar, 2 teaspoons baking powder, and 1 teaspoon salt. Combine 1 egg; 1 cup milk; and ¼ cup butter, melted; add to dry ingredients. Stir till moistened. Pour into well-greased 8x8x2-inch baking pan. Bake at 400° till golden brown, 20 to 25 minutes.

BEEF WITH RAVIOLI DUMPLINGS

3 tablespoons all-purpose flour
1 teaspoon salt
   Dash pepper
1 pound beef stew meat, cut in
   ¾ inch pieces
2 tablespoons cooking oil
¼ cup chopped onion

1 clove garlic, minced
½ teaspoon dried oregano,
   crushed
1 10-ounce package frozen peas
1 15-ounce can beef ravioli
   in sauce
2 tablespoons snipped parsley

In plastic bag combine flour, salt, and pepper. Add beef cubes, a few at a time, shaking to coat. In skillet brown meat quickly in hot oil. Add onion, garlic, and oregano; cook till onion is tender but not brown. Transfer to crockery cooker. Add 1 cup water.

Cover; cook on low-heat setting for 8 to 10 hours. Turn cooker to high-heat setting. In strainer rinse peas under hot water to separate; stir into beef mixture with ravioli and parsley. Cover and cook till heated through, about 30 minutes longer. Makes 4 servings.

A hearty dinner you can eat just 30 minutes after returning home—that's *Beef with Ravioli Dumplings.* Served directly from the cooker with cheese and breadsticks, it's a meal no one can refuse.

BARBECUE BEEF STEW

2 pounds beef stew meat, cut
  in 1-inch pieces
2 tablespoons cooking oil
1 cup thinly sliced onion,
  separated into rings
½ cup chopped green pepper
1 large clove garlic, minced
½ teaspoon salt

2 cups beef broth *or* Beef Stock
  (see recipe, page 43)
1 8-ounce can tomatoes, cut up
1 4-ounce can mushroom stems
  and pieces, drained
⅓ cup bottled barbecue sauce
3 tablespoons cornstarch
  Hot cooked rice

In skillet brown meat in hot oil. Drain off fat. Place onion rings, green pepper, and garlic in crockery cooker. Place meat atop; sprinkle with salt and ⅛ teaspoon pepper. Add beef broth, undrained tomatoes, mushrooms, and barbecue sauce; stir to mix. Cover; cook on low-heat setting for 8 to 10 hours. Turn cooker to high-heat setting. Blend ¼ cup cold water slowly into cornstarch; stir into stew. Cover and cook till thickened and bubbly, stirring occasionally. Serve over hot rice. Makes 6 to 8 servings.

SCOTTISH LAMB STEW

2 pounds lean boneless lamb
2 tablespoons cooking oil
1 medium onion, cut in wedges
1 clove garlic, minced
1 10¾-ounce can condensed
  Scotch broth soup

½ cup water
½ teaspoon dried thyme, crushed
1 8-ounce can imitation sour
  cream
2 tablespoons all-purpose flour

Cut lamb in 1-inch cubes. In skillet brown meat in hot oil. Transfer to a crockery cooker. Add onion and garlic to skillet, cook till onion is tender but not brown. Stir in soup, water, and thyme, scraping browned bits from bottom of skillet. Pour over lamb. Cover; cook on low-heat setting for 8 to 10 hours. Turn cooker to high-heat setting. Thoroughly blend imitation sour cream and flour. Slowly stir 1 cup hot liquid into sour cream; return to hot stew. Cover; cook till thickened, 15 minutes. Makes 6 servings.

TEST KITCHEN TIP—FREEZING POINTERS

To take advantage of the large quantities you can prepare in a crockery cooker, cook more food than you need for one meal and freeze the rest.

To freeze: Cool food quickly; transfer the food to a bowl set in a pan of ice water, and cool to room temperature. Immediately package in moisture-vaporproof containers allowing 1-inch headspace for expansion. Freeze.

To serve: Heat frozen food in a saucepan over low heat or in the top of a double boiler (not in slow cooker). Or bake at 400° for 1 to 2 hours.

BORSCH-STYLE STEW

1½ to 2 pounds beef short ribs,
    cut up
4 carrots, sliced (2 cups)
3 turnips, peeled, sliced, and
    cut in strips (1½ cups)
2 medium beets, peeled, sliced,
    and cut in strips (2 cups)
1 medium onion, sliced (1 cup)
1 cup sliced celery
3 cups water

1 6-ounce can tomato paste
1 tablespoon salt
1 tablespoon sugar
1 tablespoon vinegar
¼ teaspoon pepper
    • • •
1 small head cabbage, cut in
    6 wedges
Dairy sour cream

In a large skillet slowly brown the short ribs on all sides. Drain off the excess fat. Place the sliced carrots, turnips, beets, onion, and celery in a crockery cooker. Place short ribs on the vegetables. Stir together the water, tomato paste, salt, sugar, vinegar, and pepper; mix well. Pour the mixture over the ribs. Cover the crockery cooker and cook on the low-heat setting for 10 to 12 hours. Just before serving, skim the excess fat from stew.

Fifteen minutes before serving, cook cabbage wedges in a 3-quart saucepan in a large amount of boiling salted water till tender, 10 to 12 minutes. Drain cabbage well. Transfer ribs, vegetables, and cabbage to individual soup bowls. Pass sour cream to top each serving. Makes 6 servings.

GARDEN GOLD SOUP

6 medium carrots, cut up
    (about 1 pound)
3 medium potatoes, peeled and
    cubed
2 medium onions, quartered
3 stalks celery with leaves,
    cut up
4 cups water

2 teaspoons instant chicken
    bouillon granules
1 teaspoon salt
¼ teaspoon dried dillweed
    Dash pepper
¼ cup butter *or* margarine
1 cup milk
2 tablespoons all-purpose flour

Add ¼ of the vegetables and *1 cup* of the water to blender container. Cover and blend till coarsely chopped. Transfer vegetables and liquid to crockery cooker. Repeat the process 3 times, using remaining vegetables and water. Add chicken bouillon granules, salt, dried dillweed, and pepper to the cooker. Mix well. Cover and cook on the low-heat setting for 10 to 12 hours.

Place ⅓ of the cooked mixture in the blender container; cover and blend till smooth about 1 minute. Repeat process twice with remaining mixture. Or, force the hot, cooked mixture through a food mill. Return pureed vegetable mixture to crockery cooker; add the butter or margarine. Cover cooker and turn to high-heat setting. Blend milk slowly into flour; stir into hot mixture. Cover and cook till thickened and bubbly, about 30 minutes longer. Ladle into soup bowls and garnish with croutons, if desired. Makes 8 servings.

LENTIL-HAM SOUP

1 pound dry lentils (2⅓ cups)
1½ cups chopped carrot
1 cup chopped onion
1 cup chopped celery
¼ cup snipped parsley
1 teaspoon salt

¼ teaspoon dried marjoram,
   crushed
⅛ teaspoon pepper
1 bay leaf
1 meaty ham bone (about
   1½ pounds)

Place lentils in crockery cooker. Add carrot, onion, celery, and parsley. Stir in salt, marjoram, pepper, and bay leaf. Place ham bone atop. Add 7 cups water. Cover and cook on low-heat setting for 9 to 11 hours. Lift ham bone from soup. Remove meat from bone; chop meat and return to soup. Season to taste and remove bay leaf before serving. Makes 10 servings.

MEATY SPLIT PEA SOUP

1 pound ground pork
6 cups water
1 pound dry split peas
   (2¼ cups)
2 medium potatoes, peeled and
   diced (2 cups)

¾ cup chopped onion
½ cup chopped celery
2 teaspoons salt
½ teaspoon dried marjoram,
   crushed
¼ teaspoon pepper

In skillet brown ground pork; drain off fat. Transfer pork to crockery cooker. Stir in water, peas, potatoes, onion, celery, salt, marjoram, and pepper. Cover and cook on low-heat setting for 10 to 12 hours. Before serving, stir mixture; season to taste with salt and pepper. Makes 8 to 10 servings.

CREAMY BEAN SOUP

6 cups water
2 cups dry pinto beans
¼ cup chopped onion
4 teaspoons chicken-flavored
   gravy base
1 teaspoon salt

¼ teaspoon dried marjoram,
   crushed
1 cup light cream or milk
1 tablespoon all-purpose flour
6 slices bacon, crisp-cooked
   and crumbled

In saucepan bring water and beans to boiling; reduce heat and simmer, covered, 1½ hours. Pour into a bowl; cover and chill. Drain beans, reserving the cooking liquid. Transfer beans to crockery cooker. Stir in onion, chicken-flavored gravy base, salt, marjoram, and dash pepper. Add enough of the reserved cooking liquid to cover, about 2 cups. Cover and cook on low-heat setting for 12 to 14 hours. Turn to high-heat setting. Slowly blend cream into flour; stir into beans. Cover and cook till thickened and bubbly, 10 to 15 minutes. Mash beans slightly, if desired. Garnish with bacon. Makes 6 servings.

VEGETABLE-BEAN SOUP

In saucepan bring 4 cups water and 1¼ cups dry navy beans (½ pound) to boiling; reduce heat and simmer, covered, 1½ hours. Pour into a bowl; cover and chill. Drain beans; reserve liquid. Add enough water to bean liquid to make 3½ cups. Transfer beans and liquid to crockery cooker. Add 1 meaty ham bone (about 2 pounds); 2 carrots, chopped; 1 medium potato, peeled and chopped; 1 medium onion, chopped, ½ cup chopped celery; and ⅛ teaspoon pepper. Cover and cook on low-heat setting for 8 to 10 hours. Lift bone from soup; remove meat, chop, and return to soup. Mash beans slightly, if desired. Serves 6.

BEEF STOCK

Use in any recipe that calls for beef broth, or serve alone, as shown on page 32—

4 pounds beef soup bones, cut in pieces
1 cup sliced onion
½ cup chopped celery
8 whole black peppercorns
4 sprigs parsley
2 teaspoons salt
1 large bay leaf

Place soup bones in crockery cooker. Add onion, celery, peppercorns, parsley, salt, bay leaf, and 5 cups water. Cover and cook on low-heat setting for 12 to 14 hours. Remove bones. Strain broth through cheesecloth; clarify, if desired. Skim off fat. (Or, transfer to a bowl and chill. Lift off fat; leave residue on bottom of bowl for a clearer stock.) Season to taste with salt and pepper. Remove meat from bones; save meat for another use. Cover and store the meat and stock separately in tightly covered containers in the refrigerator. Makes about 4 cups beef stock and about 2 cups cooked meat.

To clarify: Crush 1 egg shell. In saucepan mix shell, 1 egg white, and ¼ cup water; add hot stock. Bring to boiling. Let stand 5 minutes; strain.

CHICKEN BROTH

Bony chicken pieces (backs, necks, and wings) from 2 chickens
1 large onion, quartered
3 whole cloves
3 stalks celery with leaves, cut up
1 carrot, quartered
1½ teaspoons salt
¼ teaspoon pepper

If desired, discard fat and skin from chicken pieces. Place chicken in a crockery cooker. Stud onion with cloves; add to cooker with celery, carrot, salt, and pepper. Add 4 cups water. Cover and cook on low-heat setting for 8 to 10 hours. Remove chicken and vegetables with a slotted spoon. Strain the broth through cheesecloth; clarify, if desired (see recipe for Beef Stock, above). Skim fat from broth. Remove any chicken from bones; save meat for another use. Cover and store meat and broth separately in tightly covered containers in the refrigerator. Makes about 4½ cups chicken broth.

BEEF GUMBO

4 cups beef broth *or* Beef Stock
  (see recipe, page 43)
1 teaspoon salt
1 teaspoon sugar
½ teaspoon paprika
½ teaspoon dried thyme, crushed
¼ teaspoon chili powder
⅛ teaspoon pepper

2 cups chopped cooked beef
1 16-ounce can tomatoes, cut up
1 10-ounce package frozen
  cut okra
1 cup chopped celery
½ cup chopped onion
2 tablespoons snipped parsley

In crockery cooker combine beef broth or Beef Stock, salt, sugar, paprika, thyme, chili powder, and pepper. Stir in cooked beef, undrained tomatoes, okra, celery, onion, and snipped parsley. Cover and cook on low-heat setting for 8 hours. Stir through soup before serving. Makes 8 to 10 servings.

BEEF AND MUSHROOMS

2 pounds boneless beef, cut in
  ¾-inch cubes
3 tablespoons cooking oil
3 medium carrots, chopped
½ cup chopped onion

1 3-ounce can sliced mushrooms,
  drained
1 teaspoon salt
1 18-ounce can tomato juice
2 tablespoons prepared mustard

In a large skillet brown beef quickly in hot cooking oil. Place carrots, onion, and drained mushrooms in crockery cooker. Add browned meat; sprinkle with salt. Combine tomato juice and mustard. Pour over meat and vegetables in cooker. Cover and cook on low-heat setting for 8 to 10 hours. Stir the soup well before serving. Ladle into soup bowls. Makes 6 servings.

BEEF-BARLEY SOUP

2 pounds beef short ribs
2 cups thinly sliced carrot
1 cup sliced celery
¾ cup chopped green pepper
1 large onion, sliced
1 16-ounce can tomatoes, cut up
⅔ cup barley

¼ cup snipped parsley
1 tablespoon instant beef
  bouillon granules
2 teaspoons salt
¾ teaspoon dried basil, crushed
5 cups water

In skillet slowly brown short ribs on all sides; drain well. In crockery cooker place carrot, celery, green pepper, and onion. Place short ribs atop. Combine undrained tomatoes, barley, parsley, bouillon granules, salt, and basil. Pour over meat. Add water; *do not stir.* Cover; cook on low-heat setting for 10 to 12 hours. Remove bones from soup; chop meat. Skim fat from soup. Return meat to cooker. Season to taste with salt and pepper. Makes 8 to 10 servings.

MULLIGATAWNY

4 cups chicken broth
2 cups chopped cooked chicken
1 16-ounce can tomatoes, cut up
1 tart apple, peeled and
    chopped
¼ cup finely chopped onion
¼ cup chopped carrot
¼ cup chopped celery

¼ cup chopped green pepper
1 tablespoon snipped parsley
2 teaspoons lemon juice
1 teaspoon sugar
1 teaspoon curry powder
2 whole cloves
¾ teaspoon salt
    Dash pepper

In crockery cooker combine chicken broth, chicken, undrained tomatoes, apple, onion, carrot, celery, green pepper, and parsley. Stir in lemon juice, sugar, curry powder, cloves, salt, and pepper. Cover and cook on low-heat setting for 8 to 10 hours. Remove cloves. Makes 6 servings.

HEARTY CHICKEN SOUP

1 16-ounce can tomatoes, cut up
1½ cups diced cooked chicken
½ cup sliced carrot
½ cup sliced celery
1 3-ounce can sliced mushrooms,
    drained

3 teaspoons instant chicken
    bouillon granules
1 bay leaf
¼ teaspoon dried thyme, crushed
5 cups water
1 cup cooked medium noodles

In crockery cooker combine undrained tomatoes, chicken, carrot, celery, mushrooms, bouillon, bay leaf, and thyme. Stir in water. Cover and cook on low-heat setting for 6 to 8 hours. Turn to high-heat setting; stir in cooked noodles. Cover; heat through, about 10 minutes. Remove bay leaf. Serves 5 or 6.

BRUNSWICK STEW

3 medium potatoes, peeled and
    cut in ½-inch pieces
1 10-ounce package frozen
    lima beans
1 10-ounce package frozen
    cut okra
1 10-ounce package frozen
    whole kernel corn
3 cups diced cooked chicken

1 tablespoon sugar
1 teaspoon salt
½ teaspoon dried rosemary,
    crushed
¼ teaspoon pepper
⅛ teaspoon ground cloves
1 bay leaf
4 cups chicken broth
1 16-ounce can tomatoes, cut up

Place potatoes and frozen vegetables in crockery cooker. Add chicken, sugar, salt, rosemary, pepper, cloves, and bay leaf. Pour chicken broth and undrained tomatoes over mixture. Cover and cook on the low-heat setting for 8 to 10 hours. Remove bay leaf and stir well before serving. Makes 10 servings.

Side Dishes and Desserts

CROCK-STYLE BEANS

8 cups water
1 pound dry navy beans (2½ cups)
4 ounces salt pork cut in small
    pieces (1 cup)

1 cup chopped onion
½ cup molasses
¼ cup packed brown sugar
1 teaspoon dry mustard

In saucepan bring water and beans to boiling; reduce heat and simmer, covered, 1½ hours. Remove from heat and pour into bowl; cover and chill. Drain beans; reserve 1 cup liquid. Transfer beans and reserved liquid to crockery cooker. Stir in pork, onion, molasses, brown sugar, and mustard. Cover; cook on low-heat setting for 12 to 14 hours. Stir. Makes 6 servings.

MAPLE-BAKED LIMAS

In saucepan bring 8 cups water and 1 pound dry lima beans (2½ cups) to boiling; reduce heat and simmer, covered, 1½ hours. Pour into bowl; cover and chill. Drain beans, reserving 1 cup liquid. Transfer beans and reserved liquid to crockery cooker. Stir in 1 cup chopped onion; 4 slices bacon, diced; ½ cup maple-flavored syrup; ½ cup catsup; 1 tablespoon Worcestershire sauce; 1 teaspoon salt; ⅛ teaspoon pepper; and 1 bay leaf. Cover; cook on low-heat setting for 8 to 10 hours. Remove bay leaf. Makes 6 servings.

BEAN POT LENTILS

1½ cups water
1 cup dry lentils (8 ounces)
½ cup chopped onion
½ teaspoon salt
1 16-ounce can tomatoes, cut up

2 tablespoons brown sugar
1 tablespoon chili sauce
½ teaspoon dry mustard
2 slices bacon, crisp-cooked
    and crumbled

In saucepan bring water, lentils, onion, and salt to boiling. Simmer, covered, 30 minutes. Transfer to crockery cooker; stir in undrained tomatoes, sugar, chili sauce, and mustard. Cover; cook on low-heat setting for 8 to 10 hours. Uncover; cook on high-heat setting for 30 minutes. Stir; top with bacon. Serves 6.

Crock-Style Beans will put you and your family in a picnic mood any time of the year. The secret of the homespun flavor is a little molasses and salt pork, then slow and easy cooking.

SWEDISH BROWN BEANS

6 cups water
1 pound dry Swedish brown beans
  (2¼ cups)
⅓ cup packed brown sugar

¼ cup vinegar
3 to 5 inches stick cinnamon
1½ teaspoons salt
2 tablespoons dark corn syrup

In saucepan bring water and Swedish brown beans to boiling; reduce the heat and simmer, covered, for 2 hours. Remove from heat and pour into a large bowl; cover and chill. Drain beans, reserving 1½ cups of the cooking liquid. Transfer beans and reserved bean liquid to a crockery cooker; stir in brown sugar, vinegar, stick cinnamon, and salt. Cover and cook on low-heat setting for 12 to 14 hours. *Stir the beans after 10 hours and again after 12 hours* to be sure beans cook evenly. To serve, remove cinnamon stick and stir in corn syrup. Mash beans slightly, if desired. Makes 6 servings.

INDIAN-STYLE BEANS AND PEPPERS

4 cups water
1½ cups dry pinto beans
  (10 ounces)
  • • •
1 16-ounce can tomatoes, cut up
¾ cup chopped green pepper

½ cup chopped onion
1 tablespoon brown sugar
1 clove garlic, minced
⅛ teaspoon pepper
3 slices bacon, crisp-cooked,
  drained, and crumbled

In saucepan bring water, beans, and 1 teaspoon salt to boiling; reduce heat and simmer, covered, 1½ hours. Pour into a bowl; cover and chill. Drain beans, reserving 1½ cups liquid. Transfer beans and reserved liquid to crockery cooker. Stir in undrained tomatoes, green pepper, onion, brown sugar, garlic, 1 teaspoon salt, and pepper. Cover and cook on low-heat setting for 12 to 14 hours. Stir through beans; top with crumbled bacon. Makes 6 servings.

ITALIAN ZUCCHINI

½ cup chopped onion
½ cup chopped green pepper
¼ cup butter *or* margarine
1 6-ounce can tomato paste
1 3-ounce can sliced mushrooms,
  drained

1 envelope spaghetti sauce mix
2½ pounds zucchini cut in
  ⅜-inch slices (8 cups)
1 cup shredded mozzarella
  cheese (4 ounces)

In a saucepan cook onion and green pepper in butter till tender but not brown. Transfer to a crockery cooker. Stir in tomato paste, drained mushrooms, *dry* spaghetti sauce mix, and 1 cup water. Add zucchini, stirring gently to coat. Cover and cook on low-heat setting for 8 hours. To serve, spoon into dishes; sprinkle with shredded mozzarella cheese. Makes 8 servings.

FRESH PEACH BUTTER

Wash 6 pounds peaches; peel, quarter, and pit. Place about *3 cups* of the peaches at a time in blender. Cover; blend till smooth. Repeat process. Measure 11 cups; place in crockery cooker. Stir in ¼ cup lemon juice and 2 teaspoons ground cinnamon. Cook, *uncovered*, on high-heat setting for 7 hours, stirring twice. Stir in 5 cups sugar. Cook, *uncovered*, 2 hours more, stirring several times. Pour into hot sterilized half-pint jars, leaving ½-inch headspace. Wipe jar rims; adjust lids. Process in boiling water bath 10 minutes (start timing when water returns to boiling). Makes 8 half-pints.

BREAKFAST PRUNES

    2 cups orange juice
    ¼ cup orange marmalade
    1 teaspoon ground cinnamon
    ¼ teaspoon ground cloves
    ¼ teaspoon ground nutmeg
    1 12-ounce package pitted,
        dried prunes (1¾ cups)
    2 thin lemon slices

In crockery cooker combine orange juice, marmalade, cinnamon, cloves, nutmeg, and 1 cup water. Stir in prunes and lemon slices. Cover and cook on low-heat setting for 8 to 10 hours. Serve warm. Makes 6 servings.

FRUIT COMPOTE SUPREME
Brighten family meals or company feasts with this colorful compote, shown on page 2—

    1 29-ounce can peach slices
    1 cup dried apricots
    ½ cup packed brown sugar
    ½ cup water
    1 teaspoon grated orange peel
    ⅓ cup orange juice
    ½ teaspoon grated lemon peel
    2 tablespoons lemon juice
    1 16-ounce can pitted dark
        sweet cherries, drained

In crockery cooker combine undrained peaches, apricots, brown sugar, water, orange peel, orange juice, lemon peel, and lemon juice. Cover; cook on low-heat setting for 9 to 10 hours. To serve, gently stir in drained cherries. Cover; cook on low-heat setting for 15 minutes longer. Makes 8 servings.

MAPLE-STEWED APPLES

    1 8-ounce package dried apples
    1 cup orange juice
    1 cup water
    ½ cup maple-flavored syrup
    1 tablespoon lemon juice

Thoroughly rinse dried apples; place in a crockery cooker. Stir in the orange juice, water, maple-flavored syrup, and lemon juice. Cover and cook on low-heat setting for 8 hours. Serve warm or chilled. Makes 6 to 8 servings.

Part-Day Cooking

(Less Than 6 Hours)

You'll enjoy entertaining guests with subtle-flavored *Lemon Chicken* prepared effortlessly in a crockery cooker (see recipe, page 60). This delicious main dish is especially good served over hot fluffy rice.

Many times your schedule requires crockery cooking recipes that will cook in just a few hours. The vast selection of recipes included in this chapter are for part-day cooking—ready in 6 hours or less. Start the food cooking and then leave to go shopping, run errands, or what- ever the activity. When you return home, the meal is ready. The crockery recipes featured here offer a host of appetizing main dishes and soups; steamed puddings and tasty quick breads; and many more inspiring crockery cooking dishes that don't take all day.

Savory Main Dishes

SPAGHETTI SAUCE ITALIANO

1 pound ground beef
½ pound bulk Italian sausage
1 28-ounce can tomatoes, cut up
2 6-ounce cans tomato paste
1 6-ounce can sliced mushrooms
1 cup chopped onion
¾ cup chopped green pepper
½ cup Burgundy
½ cup sliced pimiento-stuffed
   green olives
3 bay leaves
2 cloves garlic, minced
1½ teaspoons Worcestershire
   sauce
1 teaspoon sugar
1 teaspoon salt
½ teaspoon chili powder
⅛ teaspoon pepper
2 tablespoons cold water
2 tablespoons cornstarch
   Hot cooked spaghetti
   Grated Parmesan cheese

In skillet brown ground beef and sausage; drain off fat. Transfer to crockery cooker. Stir in undrained tomatoes, tomato paste, mushrooms, onion, green pepper, Burgundy, olives, bay leaves, garlic, Worcestershire, sugar, salt, chili powder, pepper, and ⅓ cup water. Cover; cook on high-heat setting for 5 to 6 hours. Blend water slowly into cornstarch; stir into tomato mixture. Cover; cook 10 minutes. Serve over spaghetti. Pass Parmesan. Serves 8 to 10.

RED CLAM SAUCE FOR SPAGHETTI

1 medium onion, chopped
2 cloves garlic, minced
2 tablespoons cooking oil
2 7½-ounce cans minced clams,
   undrained
1 16-ounce can tomatoes, cut up
1 12-ounce can tomato paste
¼ cup snipped parsley
1 bay leaf
1 teaspoon sugar
1 teaspoon dried basil, crushed
½ teaspoon dried thyme, crushed
½ teaspoon salt
   Hot cooked spaghetti

In skillet cook the onion and garlic in hot oil till onion is tender, 8 to 10 minutes. Transfer onion and garlic to a crockery cooker. Stir in the undrained clams, undrained tomatoes, tomato paste, snipped parsley, bay leaf, sugar, basil, thyme, and salt; mix well. Cover and cook on low-heat setting for 4 hours. Serve over hot cooked spaghetti. Makes 4 to 6 servings.

Spaghetti Sauce Italiano will rank high on your family's make-it-again-soon list. Two kinds of meat plus wine and a variety of vegetables simmer unwatched resulting in a full-flavored sauce.

TWO-MEAT SPAGHETTI SAUCE

1 28-ounce can tomatoes
1 6-ounce can tomato paste
1 medium green pepper, cut
   in pieces
1 small onion, cut in pieces
1 clove garlic
2 teaspoons sugar
1 teaspoon salt
½ teaspoon dried oregano,
   crushed
½ teaspoon dried basil,
   crushed
½ teaspoon chili powder
⅛ teaspoon pepper
2 cups cubed cooked beef *or*
   pork
1 4-ounce package sliced
   pepperoni (about 1 cup)
   Hot cooked spaghetti
   Parmesan cheese

In blender container combine un-drained tomatoes, tomato paste, green pepper, onion, garlic, sugar, salt, oregano, basil, chili powder, and pepper. Cover; blend till chopped. Pour *half* the mixture into crockery cooker. Add beef and pepperoni to remaining tomato mix-ture in blender container. Cover; blend till chopped. Add the mixture to cooker. (If blender is not used, finely chop vegetables and meats; stir in tomatoes and spices.) Cover; cook on high-heat setting for 3 to 3½ hours. Serve over spaghetti. Pass Parmesan. Serves 4 to 6.

BEEF BURGUNDY

1 2-pound beef round steak, cut
   in ¾-inch cubes
¼ cup all-purpose flour
½ teaspoon salt
3 tablespoons butter *or*
   margarine
1 cup Burgundy
¾ cup beef broth
½ cup chopped onion
1 3-ounce can whole mushrooms,
   drained
2 tablespoons snipped parsley
2 bay leaves
1 clove garlic, minced
⅛ teaspoon pepper
   Hot cooked noodles

Coat beef with mixture of flour and salt (use all flour). In skillet melt butter; brown meat on all sides. Transfer meat to crockery cooker. Combine remaining ingredients except noodles. Stir into meat. Cover; cook on high-heat setting for 3 hours. (Meat may be held another hour by turning to low-heat setting.) Remove bay leaves; discard. Serve beef over noodles. If desired, sprinkle with paprika and garnish with parsley. Makes 6 to 8 servings.

TEST KITCHEN TIP—ALL COOKERS ARE NOT ALIKE

Remember, these recipes were tested only in 3½- to 4-quart crockery cookers that have the heating element wrapped around a crockery liner. If you have a different type of cooker, you may need to adjust the timing of recipes and stir the food occasionally. See pages 4 and 5 for more information.

HOME-STYLE ROUND STEAK

1 1½-pound beef round steak
2 tablespoons all-purpose flour
2 tablespoons cooking oil
1 teaspoon instant beef
    bouillon granules
½ cup hot water

1 cup shredded carrot
1 teaspoon sugar
½ teaspoon dried thyme, crushed
2 tablespoons all-purpose flour
½ teaspoon salt
½ teaspoon Kitchen Bouquet

Cut steak into six equal pieces; coat with 2 tablespoons flour. In skillet brown in hot oil. Season with salt and pepper. Place in crockery cooker. Dissolve bouillon in hot water; combine with carrot, sugar, and thyme. Pour over steak. Cover; cook on high-heat setting for 4 hours. Remove meat to platter; keep warm. Measure liquid; add water to make ¾ cup. Pour into saucepan. Blend ¼ cup cold water into 2 tablespoons flour. Stir into liquid; add salt and Kitchen Bouquet. Cook and stir till thickened. Serve over meat. Serves 6.

MEAT LOAF FLORENTINE

1 10-ounce package frozen
    chopped spinach, thawed
2 slightly beaten eggs
1½ cups soft bread crumbs
½ cup milk
2 tablespoons soy sauce

1¼ teaspoons salt
¼ teaspoon bottled hot
    pepper sauce
2 pounds ground beef
Mushroom Sauce

Drain spinach; combine with eggs, bread crumbs, milk, soy sauce, salt, and hot pepper sauce. Add beef; mix well. Shape into round loaf slightly smaller in diameter than crockery cooker. Lay two 15x2-inch strips of foil (double thickness) crisscross fashion across bottom and up sides of cooker. Place loaf atop, not touching sides. Cover; cook on high-heat setting for 4 hours. Use foil strips as lifters to remove loaf from cooker to serving platter. Serve with Mushroom Sauce. Serves 8.

Mushroom Sauce: In saucepan combine one 3-ounce can sliced mushrooms, undrained, and 2 tablespoons all-purpose flour. Stir in 1 cup dairy sour cream and 2 tablespoons snipped chives. Cook and stir just till thickened. Do not boil. Makes 1½ cups sauce.

SMOKED BEEF AND BEAN BURGERS

Drain and slightly mash one 8-ounce can red kidney beans. Combine with one 3½-ounce package sliced smoked beef, finely snipped; ⅓ cup mayonnaise *or* salad dressing; 2 tablespoons sweet pickle relish; 1 tablespoon prepared mustard; and dash bottled hot pepper sauce. Split and toast six hard rolls. Spread about ¼ cup bean mixture on bottom half of *each* roll. Top each with 1 thin onion slice and ½ slice American cheese. Wrap each in foil; place in crockery cooker. Cover; cook on high-heat setting for 1½ hours. Makes 6.

BEEF-HAM LOAF

1 slightly beaten egg
1 10¾-ounce can condensed
    tomato soup
¾ cup coarsely crushed saltine
    crackers
⅓ cup milk

⅓ cup finely chopped onion
¼ cup snipped parsley
1½ pounds ground beef
½ pound ground fully cooked ham
• • •
Mustard Sauce

In a bowl combine egg, *half* of the soup, the cracker crumbs, milk, onion, and parsley. Add ground beef and ham; mix well. Shape meat mixture into round loaf slightly smaller in diameter than crockery cooker. Place meat loaf on rack in cooker, not touching sides. Cover; cook on low-heat setting for 6 hours. Remove loaf from cooker using two spatulas; drain off excess fat. Serve with hot Mustard Sauce. Makes 6 servings.

Mustard Sauce: In saucepan stir together the remaining soup, 1 beaten egg, 2 tablespoons prepared mustard, 2 tablespoons water, 1 tablespoon sugar, 1 tablespoon vinegar, and 1 tablespoon butter *or* margarine. Cook and stir till thickened and bubbly. Makes 1 cup.

APPLE-RAISIN TOPPED HAM

1 21-ounce can apple pie
    filling
⅓ cup light raisins
⅓ cup orange juice
2 tablespoons water

1 tablespoon lemon juice
¼ teaspoon ground cinnamon
• • •
1 1½-pound fully cooked ham
    slice (about ¾-inch thick)

Combine pie filling, raisins, orange juice, water, lemon juice, and cinnamon. Cut ham slice into six equal pieces. In crockery cooker alternately layer ham with apple mixture, ending with apple mixture. Cover; cook on low-heat setting for 4 to 5 hours. Serve with rice, if desired. Makes 6 servings.

EL PASO HAM

3 cups chopped fully cooked ham
2 cups shredded Monterey Jack
    cheese (8 ounces)
1 8-ounce can tomato sauce
1 4-ounce can green chili
    peppers, seeded and chopped

½ cup finely chopped onion
    Few drops bottled hot pepper
    sauce
    Golden Corn Bread, cut in
    squares (see recipe,
    page 38)·

In crockery cooker combine the chopped ham, cheese, tomato sauce, green chili peppers, onion, and bottled hot pepper sauce. Cover; cook the mixture on low-heat setting for 2 hours. To serve, split the hot corn bread squares. Spoon ham mixture on the bottom half of the corn bread. Cover with corn bread top; spoon more of the ham mixture over. Makes 6 servings.

TOMATO-SAUCED SPARERIBS

3 pounds lean pork spareribs
1 teaspoon salt
¼ teaspoon pepper
1 28-ounce can tomatoes
3 stalks celery, chopped

1 medium green pepper, chopped
1 medium onion, chopped
3 tablespoons cold water
2 tablespoons cornstarch
  Hot cooked rice

Cut spareribs in serving pieces. Brown in skillet. Transfer to crockery cooker; sprinkle with salt and pepper. Stir in undrained tomatoes, celery, green pepper, and onion. Cover; cook on high-heat setting for 4 hours. Lift out ribs; spoon excess fat from sauce. Blend cold water slowly into cornstarch; stir into cooker. Cook and stir till thickened and bubbly. Serve over rice. Serves 4.

BARBECUED PORK SANDWICHES

½ cup chopped onion
¼ cup chopped celery
1 clove garlic, minced
2 tablespoons butter
1 12-ounce bottle chili sauce
3 tablespoons brown sugar
2 tablespoons Worcestershire
  sauce

2 tablespoons vinegar
1 teaspoon chili powder
¼ teaspoon salt
  Dash pepper
3 cups thinly sliced cooked
  pork
1 tablespoon all-purpose flour
12 hamburger buns, split

In skillet cook onion, celery, and garlic in butter till tender but not brown. Transfer to crockery cooker. Add chili sauce, brown sugar, Worcestershire, vinegar, chili powder, salt, pepper, and ½ cup water; mix well. Stir in pork, coating all slices. Cover; cook on low-heat setting for 3 to 4 hours. Turn to high-heat setting. Blend 2 tablespoons cold water into flour; stir into pork mixture. Cover; cook 15 to 20 minutes more. Stir occasionally. Toast hamburger buns. Fill each with about ⅓ *cup* meat mixture. Makes 12.

HOT PORK-SAUERKRAUT SALAD

1 cup chopped onion
2 tablespoons cooking oil
2 cups cubed cooked pork
1 16-ounce can sauerkraut,
  drained and rinsed

½ teaspoon salt
½ teaspoon ground sage
½ cup dairy sour cream
1 large apple, cored and
  chopped

Cook chopped onion in hot cooking oil till tender but not brown. Transfer to crockery cooker. Add pork, sauerkraut, salt, sage, and 2 tablespoons water. Cover and cook on low-heat setting for 4 to 5 hours. Turn to high-heat setting. Cook 10 minutes. Stir in sour cream and apple. Cover; heat through but do not boil. Garnish with apple wedges, if desired. Makes 4 servings.

CHERRY PORK CHOPS

6 pork chops, cut ¾ inch thick
Salt
Pepper
• • •
½ of a 21-ounce can cherry pie
    filling (1 cup)

2 teaspoons lemon juice
½ teaspoon instant chicken
    bouillon granules
⅛ teaspoon ground mace
    Parsley

Trim excess fat from pork chops. In a large skillet cook the trimmings till about 1 tablespoon of fat accumulates. Discard the remaining trimmings. Brown the pork chops in the hot fat. Sprinkle each chop with salt and pepper.

In a crockery cooker stir together the cherry pie filling, lemon juice,

chicken bouillon granules, and ground mace; mix well. Place the browned pork chops atop cherry mixture. Cover and cook on low-heat setting for 4 to 5 hours. Place chops on a warm serving platter. Pour some of the cherry sauce over; pass the remaining sauce. Garnish with parsley, if desired. Serves 6.

SOUTH PACIFIC PORK ROAST

1 3-pound boneless pork
    shoulder roast
½ cup soy sauce
½ cup dry sherry
2 cloves garlic, minced

1 tablespoon dry mustard
1 teaspoon ground ginger
1 teaspoon dried thyme, crushed
    Pineapple Sauce

Place the pork shoulder roast in a clear plastic bag; set in a deep bowl. Thoroughly blend together the soy sauce, dry sherry, minced garlic, dry mustard, ginger, and thyme. Pour marinade over meat in bag; close. Place the roast in the refrigerator and marinate for 2 to 3 hours or overnight.

Transfer the pork roast and marinade to a crockery cooker. Cover and cook on high-heat setting for 3½ to 4 hours. Lift roast out onto a cutting board; let stand for 10 minutes before slicing. Discard the marinade. Arrange the sliced pork roast on a warm serving platter.

Spoon some of the hot Pineapple Sauce over the slices; pass the remaining sauce. Makes 8 servings.

Pineapple Sauce: Drain one 8½-ounce can pineapple tidbits; reserve the syrup. Add enough water to reserved syrup to make ¾ cup. In a small saucepan blend together 2 tablespoons brown sugar and 1 tablespoon cornstarch. Stir in the reserved syrup, 1 tablespoon vinegar, and 1 teaspoon soy sauce. Cook stirring constantly, till sauce is thickened and bubbly. Stir in the drained pineapple tidbits; heat through. Makes 1⅔ cups sauce.

Cherry Pork Chops simmer to perfection without any watching necessary in the crockery cooker. This enables you to concentrate on the many other details of getting ready for company.

COQ AU VIN BLANC

2 2½- to 3-pound ready-to-cook
  broiler-fryer chickens,
  cut up
¼ cup all-purpose flour
1 teaspoon paprika
½ teaspoon salt
⅛ teaspoon pepper
3 tablespoons butter, *or*
  margarine, melted
½ cup dry white wine
½ cup chicken broth

2 tablespoons chopped onion
1 tablespoon snipped parsley
¼ teaspoon dried thyme, crushed
¼ teaspoon ground sage
2 egg yolks
¼ cup milk
1 15½-ounce can boiled
  onions, drained
1 3-ounce can sliced mushrooms,
  drained
  Hot cooked noodles

Save chicken backs, necks, and wings; use in Chicken Broth (see recipe, page 43). Combine flour, paprika, salt, and pepper; coat chicken pieces thoroughly. Brown chicken on all sides in melted butter; drain well. Transfer to crockery cooker. Combine wine, chicken broth, onion, parsley, thyme, and sage. Pour over chicken. Cover; cook on low-heat setting for 5 to 6 hours. Remove chicken; pour cooking liquid into saucepan. Return chicken to cooker; cover to keep warm. Skim the excess fat from liquid. Cook the liquid till reduced to 1 cup measure, 10 to 12 minutes.

Beat egg yolks and milk together. Stir about *half* of the hot liquid into egg yolk mixture; return to saucepan. Cook and stir till mixture thickens slightly, 2 to 3 minutes. Stir in drained onions and mushrooms. Season to taste. Serve chicken over hot noodles. Pour some sauce over chicken; pass the remaining. Makes 6 servings.

LEMON CHICKEN

This great-for-company chicken dish is shown on page 50—

2 2½- to 3-pound ready-to-cook
  broiler-fryer chickens,
  cut up
¼ cup all-purpose flour
2 tablespoons cooking oil
1 6-ounce can frozen lemonade
  concentrate, thawed

3 tablespoons brown sugar
3 tablespoons catsup
1 tablespoon vinegar
2 tablespoons cold water
2 tablespoons cornstarch
  Hot cooked rice

Save chicken backs, necks, and wings; use in Chicken Broth (see recipe, page 43). Combine the flour with 1¼ teaspoons salt; coat chicken thoroughly. Brown chicken pieces on all sides in hot oil; drain. Transfer to a crockery cooker. Stir together the lemonade concentrate, brown sugar, catsup, and vinegar; pour over chicken. Cover; cook on high-heat setting for 3 to 4 hours. Remove chicken; pour cooking liquid into saucepan. Return chicken to cooker; cover to keep warm. Skim fat from reserved liquid. Blend cold water slowly into cornstarch; stir into hot liquid. Cook and stir till thickened and bubbly. Serve chicken with gravy over hot cooked rice. Makes 6 servings.

SAUCY CHICKEN AND HAM

2 2½- to 3-pound ready-to-cook
   broiler-fryer chickens,
   cut up
2 tablespoons cooking oil
1 cup fully cooked ham
   cut in strips

1 medium onion, quartered
2 tomatoes
1 11-ounce can condensed
   Cheddar cheese soup
½ teaspoon dried basil, crushed
¼ cup all-purpose flour

Save chicken backs, necks, and wings; use in Chicken Broth (see recipe, page 43). Season chicken with salt and pepper. In skillet brown chicken on all sides in hot oil; drain. Transfer to crockery cooker. Add ham and onion. Peel and chop *one* tomato; set other aside to cut in wedges for garnish. Combine chopped tomato, soup, and basil; pour over meat. Cover; cook on high-heat setting for 3 to 4 hours. Remove chicken; pour cooking liquid into saucepan. Return chicken to cooker; cover. Skim fat from liquid. Blend ½ cup cold water into flour; stir into hot liquid. Cook and stir till thickened. Serve sauce with chicken. Garnish with reserved tomato wedges. Serves 6.

CHICKEN OAHU

2 2½- to 3-pound ready-to-cook
   broiler-fryer chickens,
   cut up
¼ cup all-purpose flour
½ teaspoon paprika
½ teaspoon salt
   Dash pepper

¼ cup cooking oil
4 cups herb-seasoned stuffing
   cubes
1 8¼-ounce can crushed
   pineapple
   Oahu Sauce

Save chicken backs, necks, and wings; use in Chicken Broth (see recipe, page 43). Mix flour, paprika, salt, and pepper; coat chicken. Brown chicken in hot oil; drain. In crockery cooker combine stuffing cubes and undrained pineapple; place chicken atop. Cover; cook on low-heat setting for 6 hours. Place chicken on platter; spoon Oahu Sauce atop. Spoon stuffing into bowl; pass. Serves 6.

Oahu Sauce: In saucepan combine 1½ cups finely chopped celery, ½ cup finely chopped onion, ½ cup water, and 2 tablespoons finely chopped green pepper. Cover; simmer till tender, 12 to 15 minutes. Add one 10¾-ounce can condensed cream of mushroom soup, ½ cup dairy sour cream, and 1 tablespoon soy sauce; heat through (do not boil). Makes 3 cups sauce.

TEST KITCHEN TIP—TO INCREASE COOKING TIME

Many of your favorite "part-day" recipes can be cooked all day by reducing the temperature. For comparable results, cook foods on the low-heat setting twice as long as you would on the high-heat setting.

BEER-BRAISED RABBIT

1 2- to 2½-pound dressed rabbit,
   cut up *or* 1 2- to 2½-pound
   ready-to-cook broiler-fryer
   chicken, cut up
2 tablespoons cooking oil
3 medium potatoes, peeled and
   halved
3 or 4 carrots, bias-cut
   in 1-inch pieces

1 onion, thinly sliced
1 cup beer
¼ cup chili sauce
1 tablespoon brown sugar
1 clove garlic, minced
⅓ cup cold water
3 tablespoons all-purpose flour
½ teaspoon salt

Season meat with salt and pepper. Brown on all sides in hot oil; drain. In a crockery cooker place potatoes, carrots, and onion; place meat atop. Combine beer, chili sauce, brown sugar, and garlic. Pour over meat. Cover; cook on high-heat setting for 3½ to 4 hours. Remove meat. Drain vegetables; reserve cooking liquid. Return meat and vegetables to cooker; cover. Measure liquid; add beer or water if needed, to make 1½ cups. In saucepan slowly blend cold water into flour; stir in reserved liquid and ½ teaspoon salt. Cook, stirring constantly, till thickened. Place meat and vegetables on platter. If desired, sprinkle with paprika and garnish with parsley. Pass gravy. Serves 4.

CHICKEN AND CORNMEAL DUMPLINGS

1 9-ounce package frozen cut
   green beans
2 cups cubed cooked chicken
2 cups diced potatoes
1 13¾-ounce can chicken broth
1 12-ounce can vegetable juice
   cocktail (1½ cups)
½ cup sliced celery
½ cup chopped onion

1 teaspoon chili powder
½ teaspoon salt
6 drops bottled hot pepper sauce
1¼ cups packaged biscuit mix
⅓ cup yellow cornmeal
1 cup shredded sharp American
   cheese (4 ounces)
2 tablespoons snipped parsley
⅔ cup milk

Thaw beans by placing in strainer; run hot water over beans. Transfer to crockery cooker. Add chicken, potatoes, chicken broth, vegetable juice, celery, onion, chili powder, salt, and hot pepper sauce. Cover; cook on low-heat setting for 4 hours. Turn to high-heat setting; heat till bubbly. Combine biscuit mix, cornmeal, ½ *cup* cheese, and parsley. Add milk; stir just till moistened. Drop dough by tablespoonful onto stew. Cover; cook 45 minutes more (do not lift cover). Sprinkle dumplings with remaining cheese. Serves 4 to 6.

Beer-Braised Rabbit is a hearty one-pot meal that will cook in an afternoon while you're away from home. Potatoes and carrots share the subtly beer-flavored cooking broth that becomes a gravy.

SPANISH-STYLE CHICKEN

1 cup chopped onion
½ cup chopped celery
2 2½- to 3-pound ready-to-cook
  broiler-fryer chickens,
  cut up
1 16-ounce can tomatoes, cut up
1 clove garlic, minced

2 teaspoons instant beef
  bouillon granules
1 teaspoon paprika
1 12-ounce package fully cooked
  smoked sausage links
3 tablespoons all-purpose flour
  Saffron Rice with Peas

In a crockery cooker place onion and celery. Save chicken backs, necks, and wings; use in Chicken Broth (see recipe, page 43). Sprinkle remaining chicken with salt and pepper; place in cooker. Combine undrained tomatoes, garlic, bouillon, and paprika; pour over chicken. Cover; cook on high-heat setting for 2 to 3 hours. Place sausages atop chicken; cover and continue cooking for 1 hour more. Remove meat and vegetables to platter; keep warm. Skim fat from cooking liquid. Slowly blend ⅓ cup cold water into flour; add ½ tea-spoon salt. Stir into liquid. Cook and stir on high-heat setting till thickened and bubbly, about 15 minutes. Serve over chicken and Saffron Rice with Peas. Makes 6 servings.

Saffron Rice with Peas: In saucepan combine 2 cups water, 1 cup regular rice, ½ teaspoon salt, and ¼ teaspoon ground saffron; cover. Bring to boiling; reduce heat. Continue cooking till tender, 14 minutes. Meanwhile, cook one 10-ounce package frozen peas according to package directions; drain. Stir into rice mixture. Makes 3 cups.

BRATWURST WITH APPLE KRAUT

4 tart apples, peeled, cored,
  and sliced (3 cups)
1 27-ounce can sauerkraut,
  drained and snipped

1 pound bratwurst links,
  halved crosswise
¼ cup packed brown sugar
1 teaspoon caraway seed

In a crockery cooker stir together all ingredients. Stir in ¼ cup water. Cover and cook on low-heat setting for 3 to 4 hours. Makes 6 servings.

SAUSAGE-GARBANZO BAKE

2 15-ounce cans garbanzo
  beans, drained
1 pound Polish sausage, sliced
1 15-ounce can tomato sauce
1 cup chopped onion
¼ cup water

2 bay leaves
1 clove garlic, minced
1 teaspoon dried oregano,
  crushed
½ teaspoon ground cumin
⅛ teaspoon pepper

In crockery cooker combine all ingredients. Cover; cook on high-heat setting for 3 to 4 hours. Season to taste; remove bay leaves. Makes 4 or 5 servings.

HAWAIIAN SAUSAGE COMBO

1 20-ounce can pineapple chunks
  (juice pack)
1 17-ounce can sweet potatoes,
  sliced 1-inch thick
1 12-ounce package fully cooked
  smoked sausage links

3 tablespoons brown sugar
2 tablespoons cornstarch
¼ teaspoon salt
1 tablespoon butter *or*
  margarine

Drain pineapple, reserving the juice. Add water to juice to make 1 cup; set aside. In crockery cooker place drained pineapple, potatoes, and sausage. In saucepan stir together the brown sugar, cornstarch, and salt. Gradually blend in the reserved juice. Cook and stir till thickened and bubbly; cook and stir 1 minute more. Remove from heat; stir in butter or margarine. Pour sauce over mixture in cooker. Cover and cook on high-heat setting for 3 hours. Skim off excess fat. Stir carefully before serving. Makes 4 to 6 servings.

SAUSAGE-LAMB CASSOULET

3 15-ounce cans great northern
  beans, drained
1 cup dry white wine
1 8-ounce can tomato sauce
2 bay leaves
1 clove garlic, minced
1 tablespoon snipped parsley
½ teaspoon dried thyme,
  crushed

8 ounces boneless lamb, cut in
  ½-inch pieces
¾ cup chopped onion
2 tablespoons cooking oil
8 ounces Polish sausage, sliced
  ½ inch thick
• • •
¼ cup cold water
2 tablespoons all-purpose flour

In a crockery cooker combine beans, wine, tomato sauce, bay leaves, garlic, parsley, and thyme. In saucepan cook lamb and onion in hot oil till lamb is well browned on all sides; drain. Stir lamb, onion, and sliced sausage into bean mixture. Cover; cook on low-heat setting for 5 to 6 hours. Turn to high-heat setting. Heat till bubbly (do not lift cover). Slowly blend the cold water into flour; stir into meat-bean mixture. Cover; cook till slightly thickened. Before serving, remove bay leaves and discard. Makes 6 to 8 servings.

TEST KITCHEN TIP—CARE OF CROCKERY COOKER

Ceramic liners are more delicate than they look, and sudden temperature changes can damage them. So, do not put cold food in a hot cooker, never put your cooker in the refrigerator, and never immerse cooker or cord in water.

Clean the liner with a soft cloth and soapy water—avoid abrasive cleaners and cleansing pads. For easiest clean-up, add warm water to cooker just after removing food rather than waiting till it cools and food cooks on.

Lamb-Stuffed Grape Leaves features a seasoned-with-mint filling that is tucked inside fresh or canned grape leaves. To win even more compliments, serve them with an elegant Egg Lemon Sauce.

LAMB-STUFFED GRAPE LEAVES

1 beaten egg
¼ cup regular rice
¼ cup finely chopped onion
2 tablespoons snipped fresh
    mint leaves *or* 1 tablespoon
    dried mint, crushed

2 tablespoons snipped parsley
1 teaspoon salt
½ pound ground lamb
24 fresh *or* canned grape leaves
2 tablespoons butter, melted
    Egg Lemon Sauce

Combine egg, rice, onion, mint, parsley, ¼ *teaspoon* of salt, 3 tablespoons water, and dash pepper. Add lamb; mix well. Rinse fresh grape leaves; drain and open flat. Spoon *1 tablespoon* filling in center of each leaf. Fold in sides; roll up. Line crockery cooker with double thickness of cheesecloth. Place stuffed leaves in cooker. Mix butter, remaining ¾ teaspoon salt, and 2 cups water; pour over grape leaves. Tie corners of cheesecloth together. Cover; cook on high-heat setting for 2½ hours. Remove

bag; pour liquid into bowl, reserving ½ cup. Return bag to cooker; cover. Prepare Egg Lemon Sauce. Place stuffed leaves on platter; garnish with cherry tomatoes and fresh grape leaves, if desired. Serve hot with sauce. Serves 4.

Egg Lemon Sauce: Beat 1 egg white till stiff peaks form. Beat 1 egg yolk till light and lemon-colored. Fold egg yolk into white. Slowly stir in 2 tablespoons lemon juice. Gradually add ½ cup reserved cooking liquid. Cook and stir till slightly thickened, 5 minutes.

FISH FILLETS FLORENTINE

4 fresh *or* frozen flounder
   fillets *or* other fish
   fillets (1½ pounds)
1 10-ounce package frozen
   chopped spinach
1 3-ounce package cream
   cheese, softened

1 tablespoon lemon juice
1 tablespoon instant minced
   onion
1 11-ounce can condensed
   Cheddar cheese soup
   Ground nutmeg

Thaw frozen fillets. Cook spinach according to package directions; drain. Combine spinach, cream cheese, lemon juice, and onion; mix well. Spread about *one-fourth* of the spinach mixture on each fillet. Roll up; secure with wooden pick. Spoon soup into crockery cooker. Place fish on 12x12-inch piece of cheesecloth. Bring edges over fish; tie securely. Place in cooker. Cover; cook on low-heat setting for 4 hours. Carefully lift cheesecloth bag from cooker. Transfer fish to serving platter; remove picks. Stir sauce; pour some over fish rolls. Sprinkle with nutmeg. Pass remaining sauce. Serves 4.

SALMON LOAF

1 16-ounce can salmon
2 beaten eggs
1½ cups soft bread crumbs
¼ cup finely chopped onion
2 tablespoons butter *or*
   margarine, melted

1 tablespoon snipped parsley
1 tablespoon lemon juice
¼ teaspoon salt
   Dash cayenne
½ cup shredded sharp American
   cheese (2 ounces)

Drain salmon; reserve juices. If necessary, add water to make ¼ cup liquid. Combine liquid with remaining ingredients except the salmon and cheese. Flake salmon; stir into mixture. Shape into round loaf slightly smaller in diameter than crockery cooker. Line cooker with foil to come up 2 or 3 inches on sides. Place loaf on foil, not touching sides. Cover; cook on low-heat setting for 5 hours. Top with cheese the last 5 minutes. Makes 6 servings.

SWEETBREAD SUPPER

In crockery cooker place 1 pound beef sweetbreads, 4 cups water, 1 tablespoon vinegar, and ½ teaspoon salt. Cover; cook on low-heat setting for 4 to 5 hours. Drain sweetbreads. Remove white membrane; cube. In saucepan melt ¼ cup butter *or* margarine. Add ¼ cup chopped celery and 2 tablespoons finely chopped onion; cook till tender. Blend in ¼ cup all-purpose flour and ¼ teaspoon salt. Add 1 cup chicken broth and 1 cup milk all at once. Cook and stir till bubbly. Stir in sweetbreads; one 2-ounce jar pimiento, drained and chopped; and 2 teaspoons lemon juice. Heat through. Heat 12 frozen waffles according to package directions. Serve sweetbreads over waffles. Serves 6.

BEEF AND CARROT STEW

2 tablespoons butter *or* margarine
2 tablespoons all-purpose flour
1 8-ounce can tomato sauce
½ cup Burgundy

• • •

2 cups cubed cooked beef
1 16-ounce can sliced carrots

1 tablespoon instant minced onion
1 teaspoon sugar
½ teaspoon salt
½ teaspoon dried thyme, crushed
¼ teaspoon garlic salt
⅛ teaspoon ground cinnamon
Hot cooked noodles

In saucepan melt butter; blend in flour. Stir in tomato sauce and Burgundy; cook and stir till thickened and bubbly. Transfer to crockery cooker. Stir in beef, carrots, onion, sugar, salt, thyme, garlic salt, and cinnamon. Cover; cook on low-heat setting for 4 hours. Serve over cooked noodles. Serves 4 to 6.

SPICY SAUSAGE-BEAN SOUP

2 15-ounce cans great northern beans
1 16-ounce can tomatoes, cut up
1 4-ounce package sliced pepperoni, cut up

¾ cup chopped onion
½ cup chopped green pepper
1 clove garlic, minced
½ teaspoon salt

In a crockery cooker combine undrained northern beans and tomatoes. Stir pepperoni, onion, green pepper, garlic, and salt into the bean mixture. Pour 2 cups water over the mixture in cooker. Cover and cook on high-heat setting for 3 to 4 hours. Just before serving, spoon off excess fat. Serves 6.

MEXICAN RICE-AND-BEAN SOUP

½ cup chopped onion
⅓ cup chopped green pepper
1 clove garlic, minced
1 tablespoon cooking oil

• • •

1 4-ounce package sliced dried beef
1 18-ounce can tomato juice (2⅓ cups)

1 15½-ounce can red kidney beans
1½ cups water
½ cup regular rice
1 teaspoon paprika
½ to 1 teaspoon chili powder
½ teaspoon salt
Dash pepper

In skillet cook onion, green pepper, and garlic in hot oil till vegetables are tender but not brown. Transfer to crockery cooker. Cut beef into strips; add to onion mixture with tomato juice, undrained beans, water, rice, paprika, chili powder, salt, and pepper. Stir to mix. Cover and cook on low-heat setting for 6 hours. Stir again before serving. Makes 6 servings.

PEPPY BURGER-VEGETABLE SOUP

½ pound ground beef
½ cup chopped onion
½ cup chopped celery
• • •
1 16-ounce can tomatoes, cut up
2 cups diced potatoes
1 8-ounce can cut green beans

1 teaspoon chili powder
½ teaspoon salt
½ teaspoon Worcestershire sauce
Dash cayenne
1 10½-ounce can condensed
beef broth

In skillet brown ground beef with onion and celery; drain off fat. Transfer to crockery cooker. Stir in undrained tomatoes, potatoes, green beans, chili powder, salt, Worcestershire, and cayenne. Add beef broth and 1 soup can of water. Cover; cook on high-heat setting for 4 hours. Stir before serving. Serves 6.

BEEF-CORN CHOWDER

1 pound ground beef
½ cup chopped onion
3 cups diced potatoes
1 17-ounce can cream-style corn
1 10½-ounce can condensed
beef broth

¾ cup water
¼ teaspoon salt
¼ teaspoon dried basil, crushed
Dash pepper
Shredded sharp American cheese

In skillet brown beef and onion; drain. Transfer to crockery cooker. Stir in remaining ingredients except cheese. Cover; cook on high-heat setting for 3 to 4 hours. Stir before serving. Pass cheese to sprinkle atop. Serves 6 to 8.

VEGETABLE-BEEF SOUP

3 pounds beef shank cross cuts
1 16-ounce can tomatoes, cut up
1 10¾-ounce can tomato soup
⅓ cup chopped onion
3 cups water
2 bay leaves
1 tablespoon salt
2 teaspoons Worcestershire
sauce

¼ teaspoon chili powder
1 16-ounce can lima beans,
drained
1 8¾-ounce can whole kernel
corn, undrained
1 cup thinly sliced carrots
1 cup diced potatoes
1 cup diced celery

In a crockery cooker place beef shanks. Add undrained tomatoes, tomato soup, and onion. Combine water, bay leaves, salt, Worcestershire, and chili powder; pour over beef. Cover; cook on low-heat setting for 4 hours. Turn cooker to high-heat setting. Remove beef; discard bay leaves. Stir the remaining vegetables into soup. Cover cooker and continue cooking. Cut meat from bone; dice and return to cooker. Cover; cook for 2 to 3 hours longer. Serves 12.

BEEFY MOSTACCIOLI STEW

1½ pounds beef stew meat, cut in
   1-inch pieces
   Cooking oil
1 16-ounce can tomatoes, cut up
1 cup sliced onion
½ cup chopped carrot
½ cup sliced celery

1½ cups water
1½ teaspoons salt
1 teaspoon paprika
½ teaspoon chili powder
⅛ teaspoon pepper
1 cup uncooked mostaccioli
   Shredded mozzarella cheese

In skillet brown *half* of the meat at a time in hot oil. Drain off excess fat. In crockery cooker place undrained tomatoes, onion, carrot, and celery. Place meat atop vegetables. Combine water, salt, paprika, chili powder, and pepper; mix well and pour over meat. Cover; cook on high-heat setting for 4 hours. Cook mostaccioli according to package directions; drain well and stir into stew mixture. Pass mozzarella to sprinkle atop. Serves 4 to 6.

TURKEY-ZUCCHINI SOUP

1 8-ounce package frozen
   cut green beans
2 cups thinly sliced zucchini
2 cups chopped cooked turkey
1 8-ounce can tomato sauce
½ cup finely chopped onion
1 tablespoon instant chicken
   bouillon granules

1 teaspoon Worcestershire
   sauce
¾ teaspoon salt
½ teaspoon dried savory,
   crushed
   Dash pepper
1 3-ounce package cream
   cheese, softened

Thaw green beans by placing in strainer; run hot water over beans. In crockery cooker stir together beans, zucchini, turkey, tomato sauce, onion, bouillon, Worcestershire, salt, savory, pepper, and 4 cups water. Cover; cook on high-heat setting for 2 to 3 hours. Blend about 1 cup hot soup liquid into cream cheese; return to cooker, stirring well. Heat through. Makes 6 to 8 servings.

SENEGALESE SOUP

Serve this creamy soup as an appetizer or in cups instead of your afternoon tea—

2 10¾-ounce cans condensed
   cream of chicken soup
1 13-ounce can evaporated milk
½ cup applesauce

¼ cup shredded coconut
1 to 1½ teaspoons curry powder
¾ teaspoon garlic salt
½ teaspoon onion powder

In crockery cooker stir together soup, evaporated milk, applesauce, coconut, curry, garlic salt, onion powder, and 1 cup water; mix well. Cover; cook on low-heat setting for 4 hours. Stir before serving. If desired, pass chopped peanuts or toasted coconut to sprinkle atop each serving. Serves 5 or 6.

CLAM-VEGETABLE SOUP

Keep these ingredients on hand ready for a day that demands a no-time-to-shop meal—

In crockery cooker stir together one 28-ounce can tomatoes, cut up and undrained; one 16-ounce package frozen loose-pack hash brown potatoes (4 cups); one 10-ounce package frozen peas and carrots; 1½ cups water; 1 tablespoon instant minced onion; 2 teaspoons dried parsley flakes, crushed; 1½ teaspoons salt; and 1½ teaspoons dried marjoram, crushed. Cover and cook on high-heat setting for 3 hours.

Stir in two 7½-ounce cans minced clams, undrained; heat through, about 10 minutes. Makes 10 servings.

SHRIMP À LA CREOLE

In a crockery cooker stir together one 28-ounce can tomatoes, cut up and undrained; ½ cup chopped onion; ½ cup chopped green pepper; 2 bay leaves; 1 clove garlic, minced; 1 teaspoon dried oregano, crushed; 1 teaspoon dried thyme, crushed; ½ teaspoon salt; and 2 dashes bottled hot pepper sauce; mix well. Cover and cook on high-heat setting for 3 hours. Stir in 10 ounces frozen shelled shrimp. Cover and cook 20 minutes longer.

Slowly blend 1 tablespoon cold water into 1 tablespoon cornstarch. Stir into shrimp mixture. Cook 10 minutes more, stirring occasionally. Serve over hot cooked rice. Garnish with snipped parsley, if desired. Makes 4 servings.

The special blend of flavors typical in *Shrimp à la Creole* will develop during the long crockery simmering of this herb-seasoned sauce. Since the shrimp cook quickly, add them later.

From Vegetables to Desserts

HERBED POTATOES

1½ pounds small new potatoes
¼ cup water
¼ cup butter *or* margarine,
    melted
3 tablespoons snipped parsley

1 tablespoon lemon juice
1 tablespoon snipped chives
2 heads fresh dill, snipped
    Salt
    Pepper

Wash potatoes, peel strip from around the center of each potato. Place the potatoes in a crockery cooker; add water. Cover and cook on high-heat setting for 2½ to 3 hours. Drain well.

In saucepan heat butter with parsley, lemon juice, chives, and dill. Pour mixture over potatoes; toss till thoroughly coated. Season to taste with salt and pepper. Makes 6 servings.

CORN-STUFFED ONIONS

8 medium onions
    Salt
1 16-ounce can whole kernel
    corn, drained
2 tablespoons chopped pimiento
2 tablespoons butter *or*
    margarine

2 tablespoons all-purpose flour
½ teaspoon salt
    Dash pepper
1 cup milk
1 cup shredded sharp American
    cheese (4 ounces)

Remove centers from onions; chop enough of the centers to make 1 cup (save remaining centers for another purpose). Salt onion cavities. Combine corn and pimiento; divide into onion shells. Reserve any remaining corn. Wrap each onion securely in foil. Pour ¼ cup water into crockery cooker. Stack onions in cooker. Cover; cook on high-heat setting for 4 to 5 hours.

Just before serving, prepare sauce. In a medium saucepan over moderate heat cook the reserved cup of chopped onion in butter till tender but not brown, about 5 minutes. Stir in flour, ½ teaspoon salt, and pepper. Add milk all at once; cook and stir till thickened and bubbly. Add any reserved corn; return sauce to bubbling. Add cheese, stirring till melted. Remove onions from cooker using tongs; unwrap and place on a serving dish. Pour some of the hot cheese sauce over onions; pass remaining sauce. Makes 8 servings.

Herbed Potatoes are a delicious addition to dinner. Serve new potatoes in a delicate butter sauce seasoned with fresh dill, parsley, and chives for a special dish that's sure to please.

SHAKER-STYLE CREAMED ONIONS

2 pounds small onions, peeled
Salt
½ cup light raisins
2 tablespoons butter *or*
    margarine

2 tablespoons all-purpose flour
¾ teaspoon salt
⅛ teaspoon ground nutmeg
    Dash white pepper
1⅔ cups milk

Place onions in a crockery cooker. Sprinkle with salt; add 2 cups water. Cover and cook on high-heat setting for 3 hours. Drain onions well. Just before serving, cover raisins with very hot water and soak for 5 minutes; drain. In saucepan melt butter; stir in flour, ¾ teaspoon salt, nutmeg, and pepper. Add milk and raisins all at once; cook and stir till mixture is thickened and bubbly. Stir in cooked onions. Makes 6 to 8 servings.

COCKTAIL STEWED TOMATOES

Delicious served as a side dish, or made into a tangy tomato juice—

6 to 8 medium tomatoes
    (2 pounds)
¼ cup chopped celery
2 tablespoons chopped onion
1 tablespoon lemon juice
¾ teaspoon sugar

½ teaspoon salt
½ teaspoon prepared horseradish
½ teaspoon Worcestershire
    sauce
1 or 2 drops bottled hot pepper
    sauce

Wash, peel, and core tomatoes. Place in crockery cooker. Add remaining ingredients; stir to combine. Cover and cook on low-heat setting for 4 to 6 hours. Turn to high-heat setting; bring to boiling. Remove lid and cook 30 minutes longer. Makes 4 cups.

Tomato Juice: Place cooked tomato mixture in blender; cover and puree. Strain and chill. Makes 3 cups.

CREAM OF CELERY SOUP

2 cups Chicken Broth (see
    recipe, page 43)
1½ cups finely chopped celery
⅓ cup finely chopped onion

¼ teaspoon salt
2 cups light cream
¼ cup all-purpose flour

In crockery cooker combine Chicken Broth, celery, onion, and salt. Cover and cook on the low-heat setting for 4 to 6 hours.

Turn cooker to high-heat setting; do not remove cover. Heat till bubbly. Blend ½ *cup* of the cream slowly into the flour; stir into broth in cooker along with remaining 1½ cups cream. Cook, covered, till heated through and slightly thickened, about 30 minutes. Season to taste with salt and pepper. If desired, top each serving with a pat of butter *or* margarine and garnish with a sprinkling of paprika *or* snipped parsley. Makes 6 servings.

RATATOUILLE

1¾ cups coarsely chopped onion
1 clove garlic, minced
2 tablespoons cooking oil
4 medium tomatoes, peeled
  and coarsely chopped
½ pound zucchini, cut in
  ½-inch strips
½ pound eggplant, cut in
  ½-inch strips

2 medium green peppers, cut in
  ½-inch strips
1½ teaspoons salt
2 or 3 fresh basil leaves,
  snipped, *or* 1 teaspoon
  dried basil, crushed
2 sprigs fresh thyme, snipped,
  or ½ teaspoon dried thyme,
  crushed

In a large skillet cook onion and garlic in hot oil till tender but not brown. Transfer the mixture to a crockery cooker. Add tomatoes, zucchini, eggplant, green peppers, salt, basil, thyme, and a dash of pepper; stir to combine. Cover and cook on high-heat setting for 3 to 4 hours. Serve as a hot vegetable, or chill and serve as a salad in sauce dishes. Makes 6 to 8 servings.

GINGER-BEAN BAKE

2 teaspoons instant minced
  onion
¼ cup water
2 16-ounce cans pork and beans
  in tomato sauce

½ cup finely crushed gingersnaps (7 cookies)
¼ cup catsup
2 tablespoons light molasses

Place onion and water in a crockery cooker; let stand for 5 minutes. Add pork and beans, crushed gingersnaps, catsup, and molasses; stir to combine. Cover and cook on low-heat setting for 3 to 4 hours. Makes 6 servings.

APPLE-FILLED SQUASH

2 small acorn squash (about
  1 pound each)
2 medium baking apples, peeled
  and chopped
½ cup packed brown sugar

Ground cinnamon *or* ground
  nutmeg
Lemon juice
4 tablespoons butter *or*
  margarine

Cut squash in half lengthwise; remove seeds. Sprinkle cavities with salt. Divide chopped apple evenly among the squash halves. Sprinkle *each* half with about *2 tablespoons* of brown sugar, a dash of cinnamon or nutmeg, and a few drops of lemon juice. Dot each with *1 tablespoon* of butter. Wrap each squash half securely in foil. Pour ¼ cup water into crockery cooker. Stack the squash, cut side up, in cooker. Cover; cook on low-heat setting for 5 hours. Unwrap; place squash on serving platter. Drain any syrup remaining in foil into small pitcher; serve with squash. Makes 4 servings.

BOSTON BROWN BREAD

½ cup whole wheat flour
¼ cup all-purpose flour
¼ cup yellow cornmeal
½ teaspoon baking powder
¼ teaspoon baking soda
¼ teaspoon salt

1 beaten egg
¼ cup molasses
2 tablespoons sugar
2 teaspoons cooking oil
¾ cup buttermilk *or* sour milk
2 tablespoons raisins

Stir together flours, cornmeal, baking powder, soda, and salt. Combine egg, molasses, sugar, and oil. Add flour mixture to molasses mixture alternately with buttermilk; beat well. Stir in raisins. Turn batter into two well-greased 16- ounce vegetable cans. Cover cans tightly with foil. Place cans in crockery cooker. Cover and cook on high-heat setting for 3 hours. Remove cans from cooker; cool 10 minutes in cans. Serve warm. Makes 2 loaves.

FIG-APRICOT NUT BREAD

¼ cup snipped dried apricots
1⅓ cups all-purpose flour
½ cup sugar
1 tablespoon baking powder
½ teaspoon salt

1 beaten egg
¾ cup milk
2 tablespoons cooking oil
¼ cup snipped dried figs
¼ cup chopped pecans

Pour boiling water over apricots; cool and drain. Stir together flour, sugar, baking powder, and salt. Combine egg, milk, and oil; add to dry ingredients, stirring just till smooth. Fold in apricots, figs, and nuts. Turn into 2 well-greased 16-ounce vegetable cans with wax paper lining the bottoms. Place cans in crockery cooker. Cover; cook on high-heat setting for 3½ hours. Remove cans from cooker; cool 10 minutes in cans. Cool thoroughly. Makes 2 loaves.

PUMPKIN BREAD

1 cup packed brown sugar
⅓ cup shortening
2 eggs
1 cup canned pumpkin
¼ cup milk
2 cups all-purpose flour

2 teaspoons baking powder
½ teaspoon ground ginger
¼ teaspoon baking soda
¼ teaspoon ground nutmeg
¼ teaspoon ground cloves
¾ cup raisins

Cream sugar and shortening till fluffy. Beat in eggs, one at a time. Stir in pumpkin and milk. Stir together flour, baking powder, ginger, soda, spices, and ½ teaspoon salt; add to pumpkin mixture. Beat 1 minute with electric or rotary beater. Stir in raisins. Turn into a well-greased 3-pound shortening can. Place can in crockery cooker. Cover; cook on high-heat setting for 3½ hours. Remove can from cooker; cool 10 minutes in can. Cool thoroughly. Makes 1.

GRANOLA-PRUNE BREAD

2¾ cups all-purpose flour
¾ cup sugar
4 teaspoons baking powder
1 teaspoon salt
1 teaspoon ground cinnamon
2 beaten eggs

1⅓ cups milk
¼ cup cooking oil
½ teaspoon vanilla
1 cup granola cereal
¾ cup snipped pitted dried
   prunes

Stir together flour, sugar, baking powder, salt, and cinnamon. Combine eggs, milk, oil, and vanilla. Add to flour mixture; stir just till moistened. Fold in granola and snipped prunes. Turn into a well-greased 3-pound shortening can.

Cover loosely with foil to allow for expansion of dough. Place can in a crockery cooker. Cover and cook on high-heat setting for 3½ hours. Remove can from cooker; cool 10 minutes in can. Cool thoroughly. Makes 1 loaf.

HOLIDAY CARROT PUDDING

This tempting pudding, cooked in a fluted mold, is shown on page 2—

1¼ cups all-purpose flour
1 teaspoon baking powder
½ teaspoon baking soda
½ teaspoon ground cinnamon
½ teaspoon ground nutmeg
2 eggs
¾ cup packed brown sugar
½ cup shortening

2 medium carrots, sliced
1 medium apple, peeled, cored,
   and cut in eighths
1 medium potato, peeled and
   cut in pieces
¾ cup raisins
   Cream Cheese Sauce
   Pecan halves

Stir together flour, baking powder, soda, and spices. Place eggs, sugar, and shortening in blender. Cover; blend till smooth. Add carrot to blender mixture; blend till chopped. Add apple; blend till chopped. Add potato; blend till finely chopped. Stir carrot mixture and raisins into dry ingredients; mix well. Turn into greased and floured 6-cup mold; cover tightly with foil. Place in crockery cooker. Cover and cook on high-heat setting for 4 hours. Remove from cooker. Cool 10 minutes; unmold. Drizzle some of Cream Cheese Sauce over pudding; top with nuts. Pass remaining sauce. Serves 6 to 8.

Cream Cheese Sauce: Beat one 3-ounce package cream cheese, softened; ¼ cup butter, softened; and 1 teaspoon vanilla till fluffy. Slowly beat in 1 cup sifted powdered sugar. Stir in 2 tablespoons milk; beat smooth.

TEST KITCHEN TIP—BREAD PANS

Breads and puddings can be made in a variety of containers—any heatproof utensil that fits inside your crockery cooker. Use a 3-pound shortening can, a 2-pound coffee can, a 6-cup mold, or a special pan.

DEVIL'S FOOD PUDDING

⅓ cup sugar
2 tablespoons shortening
1 egg
1 1-ounce square unsweetened
    chocolate, melted and cooled

1¼ cups all-purpose flour
1 teaspoon baking soda
½ cup buttermilk
½ teaspoon vanilla
    Ice cream *or* Satin Sauce

Cream sugar and shortening. Add egg; mix well. Beat in chocolate. Stir together flour, soda, and ¼ teaspoon salt. Add to creamed mixture alternately with buttermilk and vanilla; beat well. Divide into two well-greased 16-ounce vegetable cans. Cover tightly with foil. Place in crockery cooker. Pour ½ cup warm water around cans. Cover; cook on high-heat setting 1½ hours. Remove cans from cooker; cool 10 minutes; unmold. Serve warm with ice cream or Satin Sauce. Makes 8 servings.

Satin Sauce: Combine 2 egg yolks, ½ cup sifted powdered sugar, ½ teaspoon vanilla, and dash salt; beat till fluffy. Whip ½ cup whipping cream; fold in. Chill thoroughly. Stir before serving.

PUDDING-IN-A-SACK

2 cups all-purpose flour
1½ cups soft bread crumbs
½ cup packed brown sugar
1 tablespoon baking soda
1 teaspoon ground cinnamon
¼ teaspoon ground cloves
¼ teaspoon ground nutmeg

1 cup raisins
1 cup ground suet (5 ounces)
½ cup chopped nuts
1 5⅓-ounce can evaporated
    milk (⅔ cup)
½ cup light molasses
    Lemon Sauce

Pour 6 cups *warm* water into crockery cooker; cover and heat on high-heat setting till boiling, 40 minutes. Meanwhile, stir together flour, crumbs, sugar, soda, spices, and 1 teaspoon salt. Stir in raisins, suet, and nuts. Add milk and molasses; mix well. Line layers of cheesecloth to form a 16-inch square, ⅛ inch thick, in a 1-quart bowl. Pour in pudding; bring up edges of cloth, tie with string, allowing room for expansion. Place in boiling water. Cover; cook on high-heat setting 3 to 3½ hours.

Remove and turn out onto plate; let stand 30 minutes. Serve warm with Lemon Sauce. Makes 10 to 12 servings.

Lemon Sauce: Mix ½ cup sugar, 4 teaspoons cornstarch, dash salt, and dash nutmeg. Gradually stir in 1 cup water. In saucepan cook and stir till thickened. Stir a moderate amount of hot mixture into 2 beaten egg yolks; return to hot mixture. Cook and stir 1 minute. Remove from heat; stir in 2 tablespoons butter, ½ teaspoon grated lemon peel, and 2 tablespoons lemon juice.

Devil's Food Pudding steams in 16-ounce vegetable cans in your crockery cooker. It's a delightful dessert or coffee break treat served with scoops of ice cream, or with Satin Sauce.

APPLE HARVEST PUDDING

2 cups all-purpose flour
½ cup packed brown sugar
2 teaspoons baking powder
1½ teaspoons ground cinnamon
½ teaspoon salt
¼ teaspoon ground nutmeg

⅓ cup shortening
2 slightly beaten eggs
⅔ cup milk
3 small apples, peeled, cored, and chopped (2 cups)
Fluffy Hard Sauce

Stir together flour, sugar, baking powder, cinnamon, salt, and nutmeg. Cut in shortening till crumbly. Combine eggs and milk; add to dry ingredients, stirring just till moistened. Fold in apples. Turn into a well-greased 2-pound coffee can with waxed paper lining the bottom. Cover tightly with foil. Place can in crockery cooker. Add 1 cup warm water to cooker. Cover; cook on high-heat setting for 4 to 4½ hours. Remove can from cooker. Cool 10 minutes; unmold. Serve warm with Fluffy Hard Sauce. Serves. 8.

Fluffy Hard Sauce: Cream 2 cups sifted powdered sugar and ½ cup butter. Beat in 1 egg yolk and 1 teaspoon vanilla. Fold in 1 stiffly beaten egg white.

ORANGE-PUMPKIN CUSTARD

3 slightly beaten eggs
1 cup canned pumpkin
½ cup sugar
½ teaspoon ground cinnamon

¼ teaspoon ground allspice
¼ teaspoon grated orange peel
1 13-ounce can evaporated milk (1⅔ cups)

Combine eggs, pumpkin, sugar, cinnamon, allspice, and orange peel; stir in milk. Pour into a greased 2-pound coffee can; cover tightly with foil. Place can in crockery cooker. Pour warm water around can, 1 inch deep. Cover and cook on the high-heat setting till knife inserted off-center comes out clean, 1¾ to 2 hours. Serve custard warm or cold. Makes 6 servings.

APPLESAUCE BREAD PUDDING

3 beaten eggs
2 cups milk
1 16-ounce can applesauce
¾ cup sugar
2 tablespoons butter, melted

2 teaspoons vanilla
¾ teaspoon ground cinnamon
9 slices day-old white bread, cubed (about 7 cups)

In a large bowl combine eggs, milk, applesauce, sugar, butter, vanilla, cinnamon, and ½ teaspoon salt. Gently stir in bread cubes. Turn into a lightly greased 2-pound coffee can; cover tightly with foil. Place can in a crockery cooker. Add ½ cup warm water to cooker. Cover; cook on high-heat setting for 3 hours. Remove can from cooker; spoon pudding into serving dishes. Top with whipped cream, if desired. Makes 8 servings.

SAUCY POACHED PEARS

5 medium pears (about 2 pounds)
½ cup Burgundy
¼ cup sugar
1 tablespoon lemon juice

⅛ teaspoon ground cinnamon
⅛ teaspoon ground nutmeg
Dash salt
2 tablespoons orange marmalade

Peel fruit; core from bottom, leaving stems on. Place pears upright in crockery cooker. Stir together Burgundy, sugar, lemon juice, cinnamon, nutmeg, and salt. Blend in marmalade; carefully pour over pears. Cover and cook on the low-heat setting for 3½ to 4 hours. Serve the pears warm or chilled with syrup. Pass sour cream or whipped cream cheese, if desired. Makes 5 servings.

CRANBERRY-ORANGE RELISH

2 cups sugar
1 teaspoon grated orange peel
1 cup orange juice

1 16-ounce package fresh *or* frozen cranberries (4 cups)

In crockery cooker combine sugar, orange peel, and juice; stir till sugar is nearly dissolved. Stir in cranberries. Cover; cook on low-heat setting for 6 hours. Mash berries. Chill till served. Makes 4 cups.

MINCEMEAT-STUFFED APPLES

4 medium baking apples
½ cup prepared mincemeat
2 tablespoons chopped
   maraschino cherries

2 tablespoons chopped walnuts
2 tablespoons brown sugar
4 teaspoons water
4 teaspoons butter *or* margarine

Core apples; enlarge openings slightly. Place each apple on a 12-inch square of foil. Combine mincemeat, cherries, nuts, and sugar. Divide filling among apples. Sprinkle each apple with *1 tea-spoon* of water and dot with *1 teaspoon* of butter. Bring foil up around apples; twist ends together to seal. Place in crockery cooker. Cover; cook on low-heat setting for 5 to 6 hours. Serves 4.

SPICED PEACHES

1 29-ounce can peach halves
2 tablespoons sugar
1 tablespoon vinegar

6 inches stick cinnamon, broken
¼ teaspoon whole cloves
¼ cup brandy

In crockery cooker combine undrained peaches, sugar, vinegar, and spices. Stir to make sure syrup covers fruit. Cover; cook on low-heat setting for 4 hours. Stir in brandy. Chill 48 hours. Remove whole spices. Serves 6.

Cooking for a Crowd

Serve *Middle Eastern Sandwiches* buffet-style for a get-together (see recipe, page 88). Fill the hollow Pita bread with a seasoned meat filling, chopped lettuce, chopped tomato, cucumber, and yogurt.

Want to invite a group of friends over for an informal dinner party, potluck supper, or perhaps an after-the-game supper without a lot of work? Then get your crockery cooker out and cook the food the easy-to-prepare way. Using the pot also simplifies serving. Set the cooker on a buffet table and let people help themselves. Or, bring the slow cooker to the table—less work for the hostess and more fun for the guests. In this chapter you'll find impressive soup appetizers, sandwich fillings, hot beverages, and party fondues.

Crockery-Style Main Courses

FRUITED TURKEY ROAST

1 3-pound frozen boneless
    turkey roast, thawed
1 10-ounce jar cherry
    preserves

1 8-ounce can crushed pineapple,
    drained
2 tablespoons lemon juice
    Dash cloves

Place turkey in crockery cooker. Cover and cook on low-heat setting for 8 hours. Just before serving, prepare the sauce. In saucepan combine cherry preserves, drained pineapple, lemon juice, and cloves. Heat through.

To serve turkey warm, place the roast on a serving platter; let stand 10 minutes before carving. Spoon some of hot sauce over; pass remaining sauce.

To serve turkey cold, remove roast from cooker. Promptly refrigerate meat to cool quickly. When chilled, cover meat. Chill sauce. Slice turkey; arrange on platter. Serve sauce over slices. Makes 10 to 12 servings.

BEEF STROGANOFF

2 pounds beef sirloin steak,
    cut in thin strips
    Salt
    Pepper
3 tablespoons cooking oil
1 10½-ounce can condensed beef
    broth
1 cup chopped onion
1 6-ounce can sliced mushrooms,
    drained

½ cup water
2 tablespoons Worcestershire
    sauce
2 tablespoons tomato paste
2 cloves garlic, minced
1 cup dairy sour cream
¼ cup dry white wine
3 tablespoons cornstarch
    Hot cooked noodles

Sprinkle meat with salt and pepper. In a large skillet brown *half* the meat at a time in hot cooking oil; drain off fat. Transfer meat to crockery cooker. Stir in beef broth, onion, mushrooms, water, Worcestershire sauce, tomato paste, and garlic. Cover; cook on low-heat setting for 8 to 10 hours. To serve, turn to high-heat setting. Heat till bubbly, 15 minutes. Blend sour cream and wine slowly into cornstarch; stir into meat mixture. Cover and cook 15 minutes longer. Serve over hot noodles. Makes 8 to 10 servings.

Crockery cooking makes it easy to entertain. *Fruited Turkey Roast* cooks all day while you are away from home working or shopping. Upon returning, the meal is ready to serve your guests.

BEEF BRISKET IN BEER

1 onion, thinly sliced and
    separated into rings
1 4-pound fresh beef brisket
½ teaspoon salt
⅛ teaspoon pepper

1 12-ounce can beer (1½ cups)
¼ cup chili sauce
2 tablespoons brown sugar
1 clove garlic, minced
¼ cup all-purpose flour

Place onion rings in crockery cooker. Trim excess fat from brisket. Cut meat in half and fit into cooker atop onions. Sprinkle with salt and pepper. Combine beer, chili sauce, brown sugar, and garlic; pour over meat. Cover; cook on the low-heat setting for 10 to 12 hours. Remove beef; skim fat from liquid. Measure 1½ cups liquid; pour into saucepan. Discard remaining liquid. Return meat to cooker; cover to keep warm. Blend ½ cup cold water slowly into flour; stir into liquid. Cook and stir till thickened and bubbly. Season to taste. To serve, slice meat across the grain; pass the gravy. Serves 8 to 10.

CURRIED HAM

1 cup chopped apple (1 medium)
¾ cup chopped onion
3 tablespoons butter
2 tablespoons all-purpose flour
4 teaspoons curry powder
1 10¾-ounce can condensed
    cream of mushroom soup

2½ cups milk
6 cups cubed fully cooked ham,
    chicken, *or* turkey
1 cup dairy sour cream
  Hot cooked rice
  Snipped parsley
  Toasted slivered almonds

Advance preparation: In saucepan cook apple and onion in butter till tender. Blend in flour and curry powder. Add soup; blend in milk. Cook and stir till thickened and bubbly. Cool mixture quickly in ice water (do not stir). Refrigerate up to 24 hours.

Before serving: Transfer chilled mixture to crockery cooker; stir in meat. Cover; cook on high-heat setting for 1½ hours. (*Or*, omit chilling step; transfer soup mixture immediately to crockery cooker; stir in meat. Cover; cook on low-heat setting for 1½ hours.) Stir in sour cream. Cover; cook on high-heat setting 30 minutes longer, stirring occasionally. Serve over hot rice; garnish with snipped parsley and toasted slivered almonds. Pass other condiments such as sliced green onion, sliced preserved kumquats, raisins, and flaked coconut, if desired. Makes 12 servings.

TEST KITCHEN TIP—ALL COOKERS ARE NOT ALIKE

Remember, these recipes were tested only in 3½- to 4-quart crockery cookers that have the heating element wrapped around a crockery liner. If you have a different type of cooker, you may need to adjust the timing of recipes and stir the food occasionally. See pages 4 and 5 for more information.

FRENCH ONION SOUP

6 to 8 onions, thinly sliced
   (6 to 8 cups)
¼ cup butter *or* margarine
4 10½-ounce cans condensed
   beef broth

1 soup can water (1¼ cups)
2 teaspoons Worcestershire
   sauce
⅛ teaspoon pepper

In large skillet cook onions in butter till tender, about 20 minutes. Transfer onions and butter to crockery cooker. Add condensed beef broth, water, Worcestershire sauce, and pepper. Cover and cook on low-heat setting for 4 to 6 hours. Ladle soup into bowls; garnish with cheese crackers or slices of toasted French bread, if desired. Makes 10 to 12 servings.

SAVORY TOMATO-BEEF SOUP

1 pound beef stew meat, cut in
   ¾ inch pieces
2 tablespoons cooking oil
4 cups water
1 28-ounce can tomatoes, cut up
1 cup sliced carrot
1 cup chopped celery
¼ cup snipped celery leaves
2 teaspoons instant beef
   bouillon granules

1 teaspoon salt
½ teaspoon dried marjoram,
   crushed
½ teaspoon dried basil, crushed
¼ teaspoon dried savory,
   crushed
¼ teaspoon dried thyme, crushed
⅛ teaspoon ground mace
   Several dashes bottled hot
   pepper sauce

Trim excess fat from meat. In skillet brown meat in hot oil; drain. Transfer meat to crockery cooker. Stir in water, undrained tomatoes, carrot, celery, celery leaves, bouillon granules, salt, marjoram, basil, savory, thyme, mace, and hot pepper sauce. Cover and cook on the low-heat setting for 8 to 10 hours. Before serving, skim off fat and stir soup well. Makes 8 servings.

BEEF CHOWDER

1½ pounds ground beef
½ cup chopped celery
½ cup chopped onion
⅓ cup chopped green pepper
2 16-ounce cans tomatoes,
   cut up

2 10¾-ounce cans condensed
   cream of celery soup
1 17-ounce can cream-style corn
¼ cup snipped parsley
½ teaspoon ground thyme
¼ teaspoon salt

In skillet cook beef, celery, onion, and green pepper till meat is browned; drain well. Transfer mixture to crockery cooker. Stir in undrained tomatoes, soup, corn, parsley, thyme, and salt. Cover and cook on low-heat setting for 8 hours. Season to taste with salt and pepper. Makes 10 to 12 servings.

SPICY BEEF SANDWICHES

1 small head cabbage, shredded
(3 cups)
1 3-pound beef chuck pot roast
1 10¾-ounce can condensed
tomato soup
1 cup chopped onion
½ cup hot-style catsup
2 tablespoons sugar
2 tablespoons Worcestershire
sauce

2 tablespoons vinegar
1 bay leaf
1 clove garlic, minced
2 teaspoons chili powder
1 teaspoon dried oregano,
crushed
½ teaspoon salt
¼ cup cold water
2 tablespoons all-purpose flour
Hard rolls *or* French bread

Place shredded cabbage in crockery cooker. Trim excess fat from roast. Cut roast in half and fit into cooker atop cabbage. Combine tomato soup, onion, catsup, sugar, Worcestershire sauce, vinegar, bay leaf, garlic, chili powder, oregano, and salt; pour over meat. Cover and cook on low-heat setting for 10 to 12 hours. Lift out roast. Skim excess fat from sauce. Cover cooker; turn to high-heat setting. Heat sauce till bubbly. Meanwhile, remove meat from bone; discard bone. Cool meat slightly; slice thinly across the grain. Blend water slowly into flour; stir into sauce. Return sliced meat to cooker. Cover; cook 10 minutes longer. Serve the hot beef mixture over split hard rolls or slices of French bread. Makes 15 to 20 sandwiches.

MIDDLE EASTERN SANDWICHES

Pictured on page 82. Buy round, flat Pita bread at a delicatessen or specialty shop—

4 pounds boneless beef *or* lamb,
cut in ½-inch cubes
¼ cup cooking oil
2 cups chopped onion
2 cloves garlic, minced
1 cup dry red wine
1 6-ounce can tomato paste
2 teaspoons salt
2 teaspoons dried oregano,
crushed
1 teaspoon dried basil, crushed

½ teaspoon dried rosemary,
crushed
¼ cup cold water
¼ cup cornstarch
Pita pocket bread
2 cups shredded lettuce
1 large tomato, seeded and
diced
1 large cucumber, seeded and
diced
1 8-ounce carton plain yogurt

In skillet brown *1 pound* of the meat in *1 tablespoon* of hot oil at a time; drain. Transfer meat to crockery cooker. Add onion and garlic to skillet; cook till tender. Add to meat with wine, tomato paste, salt, oregano, basil, rosemary, and dash pepper; mix well. Cover; cook on low-heat setting for 4 hours. To serve, turn cooker to high-heat setting. Blend water into cornstarch; stir into meat mixture. Cook till thickened and bubbly, stirring occasionally. Split bread to make a pocket; fill each with meat mixture, lettuce, tomato, cucumber, and yogurt. Makes 10 to 16 sandwiches. (Depending on size of Pita loaves.)

TIJUANA SANDWICHES

3 cups chopped cooked beef
1 16-ounce can refried beans
½ cup chopped onion
½ cup chopped green pepper
⅓ cup chopped ripe olives
1 8-ounce can tomato sauce
2 teaspoons chili powder
1 teaspoon Worcestershire sauce
¼ teaspoon garlic powder
¼ teaspoon pepper
¼ teaspoon paprika
Dash celery salt
Dash nutmeg
1 cup crushed corn chips
Taco shells, heated
½ medium head lettuce, shredded
2 tomatoes, chopped
1 cup shredded sharp American
   cheese (4 ounces)
Bottled hot pepper sauce

In crockery cooker stir together cooked beef, beans, onion, green pepper, and olives. Stir in tomato sauce, chili powder, Worcestershire sauce, garlic powder, pepper, paprika, celery salt, nutmeg, ¾ cup water, and 1 teaspoon salt. Cover and cook on high-heat setting for 2 hours. Just before serving, fold in crushed corn chips. Spoon mixture into taco shells; top with lettuce, tomatoes, and cheese. Pass hot pepper sauce. Makes 12 to 15 sandwiches.

ITALIAN PORK SANDWICHES

2 pounds ground pork
1 15-ounce can tomato sauce
1½ cups chopped onion
1 8-ounce can pizza sauce
3 cloves garlic, minced
2 tablespoons vinegar
1 tablespoon Worcestershire
   sauce
1 teaspoon salt
½ teaspoon fennel seed
Few dashes bottled hot
   pepper sauce
Individual hard rolls,
   split
3 cups shredded mozzarella
   cheese (12 ounces)

In large skillet quickly brown half the pork at a time; drain well. Transfer meat to crockery cooker. Stir in tomato sauce, onion, pizza sauce, garlic, vinegar, Worcestershire sauce, salt, fennel, and hot pepper sauce. Cover and cook on low-heat setting for 8 to 10 hours. Fill hard rolls with meat mixture; sprinkle shredded mozzarella atop. Makes 15 to 20 sandwiches.

FRANKWICHES

In crockery cooker combine two 11-ounce cans condensed Cheddar cheese soup, ½ cup finely chopped onion, ½ cup sweet pickle relish, and 4 teaspoons prepared mustard. Stir in 2 pounds frankfurters, thinly sliced. (Mixture will be thick.) Cover and cook on low-heat setting; for 3 to 4 hours. Turn to high-heat setting; stir in one 8-ounce can imitation sour cream. Cover and cook 10 to 15 minutes longer, stirring occasionally. Serve over toasted English muffin halves *or* squares of hot corn bread. Makes 16 to 18 sandwiches.

Beverages and Fondues

LEMON-MAPLE WINTER NOG

5 5¾-ounce cans frozen lemon
   juice, thawed
3 cups maple-flavored syrup

1 ⁴/₅-quart bottle blended
   whiskey
Ground nutmeg

In crockery cooker combine lemon juice, syrup, and whiskey. Cover; heat on low-heat setting for 3 to 4 hours. Sprinkle with nutmeg. If desired, float lemon slices atop nog. Serve in warmed mugs. Makes 20 (4-ounce) servings.

FLAMING PUNCH

Pictured on page 2, this hot beverage warms the coldest bones—

2 ⁴/₅-quart bottles Burgundy
1 cup sugar
2 3x½-inch strips orange peel
1 cup orange juice

2 2x½-inch strips lemon peel
½ cup lemon juice
12 whole cloves
½ cup rum

In crockery cooker combine Burgundy, sugar, orange peel and juice, lemon peel and juice, and cloves. Stir to dissolve sugar. Cover; heat on low-heat setting for 4 to 6 hours. In saucepan heat rum; pour into ladle, ignite. Slowly pour into wine. If desired, float orange slices atop. Makes 16 (4-ounce) servings.

WASSAIL

1 medium orange, halved
10 whole cloves
2 ⁴/₅-quart bottles claret

½ cup sugar
4 inches stick cinnamon, broken
½ teaspoon ground ginger

Stud orange halves with cloves. Place in crockery cooker; add remaining ingredients. Stir to dissolve sugar. Cover; heat on low-heat setting for 4 hours. Remove cinnamon and orange halves. Makes 14 (4-ounce) servings.

HOT SPICED APPLE WINE

In crockery cooker combine 3 cups apple cider *or* apple juice; one ⁴/₅-quart bottle dry white wine; ¼ cup packed brown sugar; peel from ¼ lemon, cut in thin strips; 2 tablespoons lemon juice; 1½ teaspoons ground cinnamon; and ¼ teaspoon ground cloves. Stir to dissolve sugar. Cover; heat on low-heat setting for 4 to 6 hours. Serve in warmed mugs. Makes 8 to 10 servings.

GLÖGG

3 ⅘-quart bottles Burgundy
1 cup sugar
1 cup raisins
¼ cup sweet vermouth
Peel from 1 orange

8 inches stick cinnamon, broken
6 whole cardamom pods, crushed slightly
½ teaspoon whole cloves
1 cup blanched whole almonds

In crockery cooker combine Burgundy, sugar, raisins, vermouth, and orange peel. Stir to dissolve sugar. Tie the spices in a cheesecloth bag; add to wine mixture. Cover and heat on the low-heat setting for 4 to 6 hours, or on the high-heat setting for 2½ to 3 hours. Remove spices and peel; add almonds. Serve with spoons for eating almonds. Makes 20 (4-ounce) servings.

HONEY MULLED CIDER

10 cups apple cider *or* apple juice (2½ quarts)
⅓ cup honey
⅛ teaspoon salt

Dash ground ginger
Dash ground nutmeg
5 inches stick cinnamon, broken
1½ teaspoons whole cloves

In crockery cooker combine cider, honey, salt, ginger, and nutmeg. Add cinnamon and cloves (tied in cheese-cloth, if desired). Cover; heat on low-heat setting for 4 to 4½ hours. Makes 20 (4-ounce) servings.

SPICED COFFEE

⅓ cup sugar
¼ cup instant coffee crystals
1 teaspoon ground cinnamon

¼ teaspoon ground allspice
⅛ teaspoon salt
6 cups milk

In a crockery cooker combine sugar, coffee crystals, cinnamon, allspice, salt, and 1 cup water; stir to dissolve. Stir in the milk. Cover and heat on the low-heat setting for 3 to 4 hours. Makes 8 to 10 servings.

CROCKERY COCOA

3⅓ cups nonfat dry milk powder
⅔ cup unsweetened cocoa powder

½ cup sugar
1 teaspoon vanilla extract

In crockery cooker combine milk, cocoa, and sugar. Stir in vanilla and 6 cups warm water; stir to dissolve. Cover and heat on low-heat setting for 3 to 4 hours. Makes 8 to 10 servings.

Spiced Cocoa: Add 1 teaspoon ground cinnamon and ¼ teaspoon ground nutmeg to dry ingredients.
Mocha Cocoa: Add 2 tablespoons instant coffee crystals to hot cocoa.

MEXICAN FONDUE

1 17-ounce can cream-style corn
1 15-ounce can tomato sauce
   with tomato tidbits
3 tablespoons chopped canned
   green chili peppers
1 teaspoon chili powder

4 cups shredded sharp American
   cheese (16 ounces)
2 tablespoons cold water
2 tablespoons cornstarch
   French bread, cut in bite-
   size cubes, each with crust

In crockery cooker combine corn, tomato sauce, chili peppers, and chili powder; add cheese. Cover; cook on high-heat setting till cheese is melted, about 1 hour, stirring occasionally. Blend cold water slowly into cornstarch; stir into cheese mixture. Cook on high-heat setting till thickened, about 10 minutes longer, stirring often. Serve at once or reduce heat and keep warm, covered, on low-heat setting for 1 to 2 hours; stir occasionally. Spear bread cube with fondue fork; dip in fondue, swirling to coat. Serves 10 to 12.

FONDUE ITALIANO

½ pound ground beef
2 8-ounce cans tomato sauce
½ envelope spaghetti sauce mix
   (about 2 tablespoons)
3 cups shredded Cheddar cheese
   (12 ounces)

1 cup shredded mozzarella
   cheese (4 ounces)
½ cup chianti
1 tablespoon cornstarch
   Italian bread, cut in bite-
   size cubes, each with crust

In skillet brown meat; drain off fat. Transfer meat to crockery cooker. Stir in tomato sauce and spaghetti sauce mix. Gradually stir in cheeses. Cover and cook on high-heat setting till cheese is melted, 40 to 45 minutes, stirring occasionally. Blend chianti slowly into cornstarch; stir into cheese mixture. Cook on high-heat setting till thickened, about 20 minutes longer, stirring often. Serve at once or reduce heat and keep warm, covered, on low-heat setting for 1 to 2 hours; stir occasionally. Spear bread cube with fondue fork; dip in fondue, swirling to coat. Makes 10 to 12 servings.

CHOCOLATE-NUT FONDUE

1 12-ounce package semisweet
   chocolate pieces (2 cups)
1 13-ounce can evaporated milk
   (1⅔ cups)

1 cup sugar
1 cup chunk-style peanut butter
   Banana, apple, *or* marshmallow
   dippers

In crockery cooker combine chocolate, milk, sugar, and peanut butter. Cover; cook on high-heat setting for 30 minutes; stir well to blend. Serve at once or reduce heat and keep warm, covered, on low-heat setting for 1 to 2 hours; stir occasionally. Spear dipper; dip in fondue, swirling to coat. Serves 8.

Index

A-B

C-D